Praise for *Made to Move Mountains*

"Kristen is that vulnerably compassionate and fiercely courageous friend we want leading us—showing us how to be brave, how to behold with eyes of faith, and how to trust God for the impossible things he calls us to."

Ruth Chou Simons, bestselling author of *Beholding and Becoming* and *GraceLaced*; founder of GraceLaced.com

Praise for *Raising World Changers in a Changing World*

"These aren't some words on a page; these are words actually lived. Possible. Proven. These are words lived out that are literally changing the world from the inside out. The family you want is possible—and this is the book you need."

Ann Voskamp, *New York Times* bestselling author of *The Broken Way* and *One Thousand Gifts*

"In a world where it is countercultural to raise our children to live outward and not inward, Kristen Welch spurs us on in this journey of living openhearted to all that God wants to do through us. She isn't just telling us how; she is showing us by the very life her family is living today! As you read these pages, you will not only find guidance in raising children who are world changers, but you will find yourself moved to be a world changer as well!"

Ruth Schwenk, founder of TheBetterMom.com; author of *Pressing Pause* and *For Better or for Kids*

D0109805

"*Raising World Changers in a Changing World* gets to the heart of everything I have lived and believed through all the years of my ministry. Learn how to leave a legacy of faith and purpose for your children that will transform your life and theirs. Please read this book. Your life will be changed."

Sally Clarkson, author of *The Lifegiving Home*,
The Lifegiving Table, and more

"If you feel overwhelmed, get ready to be encouraged. Welch offers parents two things that are sorely lacking in our world today: hope and direction."

Heidi St. John, author, speaker, blogger,
and executive director at Firmly Planted Family

"*Raising World Changers in a Changing World* is a must-read for every Christian parent who desires for their children to burst out of the safe, predictable bubble of the American Dream and begin living a life of service that is greater than anything they could ever ask or imagine."

Erin Odom, author of *More Than Just Making It*
and *You Can Stay Home with Your Kids*;
creator of thehumbledhomemaker.com

Made to Move
Mountains

Made to Move Mountains

HOW GOD USES OUR DREAMS AND DISASTERS TO ACCOMPLISH THE IMPOSSIBLE

KRISTEN WELCH

BakerBooks

a division of Baker Publishing Group
Grand Rapids, Michigan

Published by Baker Books
a division of Baker Publishing Group
PO Box 6287, Grand Rapids, MI 49516-6287
www.bakerbooks.com

Printed in the United States of America

Library of Congress Cataloging-in-Publication Data
Names: Welch, Kristen, 1972– author.
Title: Made to move mountains : how God uses our dreams and disasters to accomplish the impossible / Kristen Welch.
Description: Grand Rapids : Baker Books, a division of Baker Publishing Group, 2020.
Identifiers: LCCN 2019028425 | ISBN 9780801075803 (paperback)
Subjects: LCSH: Power (Christian theology)
Classification: LCC BT738.25 .W45 2020 | DDC 248.4—dc23
LC record available at https://lccn.loc.gov/2019028425

Some names and details have been changed to protect the privacy of the individuals involved.

Published in association with William K. Jensen Literary Agency, 119 Bampton Court, Eugene, Oregon 97404.

20 21 22 23 24 25 26   7 6 5 4 3 2 1

Terrell, this one is for you.

Thank you for being my climbing partner
all these years.

Contents

Foreword by Ann Voskamp   11

Introduction   15

1. The Mountain in Our Way   21

2. Rejoicing in the Impossible   39

3. The Best View Means the Hardest Climb   51

4. Jesus Changes Everything   69

5. Oh, We of Little Faith   85

6. Permission to Grieve   97

7. Your Invitation to Climb   109

8. Just Keep Climbing   125

9. Rainbows in the Rain   137

10. Miracle Territory   151

11. It's Not Too Late   167

Contents

12. Do What You Can, Where You Are, with What You Have   179

13. The World Needs You   195

Epilogue: Beyond Mountains, There Are Mountains   207

Acknowledgments   211

Notes   213

Foreword

To scale that mountain ahead of you, you have to silence the lies in your head.

You know the ones.

The lie that says you should just lay down and give up—when God is giving you his hand right now to help you up.

The lie that says you don't have what it takes to keep going—when the Mover of mountains takes you, has you, and keeps you so that nothing can stop you from moving your mountain.

The lie that says the mountain you are facing is greater than the God who is facing you—when God has not turned his back on you for one moment ever so that you are facing not the insurmountable but the One who is unstoppable.

Because our God moves mountains, your mountains can move.

I count Kristen Welch as one of my closest heart sisters, a spiritual mentor, and a ministry partner, with whom I've worked closely for years to bring hope to women. I can testify: Kristen's radically surrendered life detonates doubt and bears witness to the truth—whatever mountain you are climbing can stretch out into a road because Jesus didn't climb down from the cross but stretched out his arms and made himself a way through mountains.

Kristen has bravely lived exactly this over the last decade with cruciform courage and tenacious trust. Battling through profound health obstacles, relentless ministry mountains, and heartbreaking relational inclines, Kristen has defiantly trusted God to move mountains of injustice, indifference, and inequality. I've watched Kristen lay her whole life down for God in order to knock other people's mountains down and be more than enough for her own.

God either moves mountains or carries us over to build our faith. And Kristen's story will build your faith in a God who doesn't move mountains to make things easy but moves our hearts to make everything about him.

Dare I say that the unforgettably powerful, heart-moving manifesto you are holding in your hands right now will leave you much like the people of ancient Cairo?

In the late days of the tenth century, the caliph of Cairo threw down an ultimatum to Abraam, a Christian, to literally enact the words of Matthew 17:20: "If you have faith as small as a mustard seed, you can say to this mountain, 'Move from here to there,' and it will move. Nothing will be impossible for you." And if no mountain moved? The caliph threatened to expel, enslave, or execute every Christian in the city. For three long days, the faithful prayed, fasted, and raised one unified, repeating cry, "Lord, have mercy."

The way you ask God to move your mountain is not to focus on the height of the mountain but on the depth of God's mercy.

After three days, the entire Christian community gathered at the foot of Mokattam Mountain. With the caliph of Cairo present, Abraam prayed again, "Lord, have mercy."

And the dirt beneath their bowed knees shook. The earth quaked. With thousands as witnesses at the foot of Mokattam Mountain, the mountain moved.

The believers rose to their feet—and the mountain rose right off the ground.

When your faith is grounded in Christ, mountains in your way move. And when your world is rocked, it's because God is moving your mountain.

Not once, not twice, but three times, the ancient story goes, the caliph and all who had gathered saw Mokattam Mountain lift up from the earth, sunbeams wedging in the space between, as if the mountain was suspended in light above the terra firma.

As sun rays swept under the moved mountain, the caliph looked down and saw those rays of light sweep across his feet and could only murmur, "I see."

See the light: mountains move. The light of Christ pries them out. Feel rays of hope warm your darkest places of despair.

Mountains can move, burdens can lift, and you can forge onward because Christ is lifted higher than the heights of any mountain. What is your mountain to your Savior?

You can take on any steep incline—because Jesus's heart is inclined to yours. You can scale any height—because Jesus carries the weight of your burden. He carries you. You were made to move mountains—because your heart was made to move whatever is necessary to get closer to him.

Egyptian Christian tradition says that after watching Mokattam Mountain move, the caliph of Cairo converted to Christianity.

Turn these soul-quaking pages and be converted. Turn and believe with your whole heart that you were made to move mountains.

Ann Voskamp, board member for Mercy House Global
and *New York Times* bestselling author
of *The Broken Way* and *One Thousand Gifts*

Introduction

When I sat down to write this book, I did so with excitement and direction. I had a plan.

In 2010, my family started Mercy House Global, a nonprofit that oversees three maternity centers in Kenya for young pregnant girls. We fund them through donations and the sale of fair-trade products. This has allowed us to create dignified jobs for thousands of women around the world. People started saying we were brave; I almost believed them.

I've chronicled this long, roller-coaster journey on my blog, *We Are THAT Family*, for a decade. But the more I wrote, the more emails I received with comments such as, "I could never do what you're doing," or "Wow, you keep climbing—you were made for this!" The more I read, the more I longed for readers to know the whole truth: I'm afraid of the mountain.

I'm inadequate and weak, but God is doing the impossible anyway. I wanted to write a book that would inspire, encourage, and cheer you on your own climb. I wanted to be your personal cheerleader, chanting in your ear, "Go, you! You can do it!" I dreamed of you strapping on hiking boots when you neared the last chapter because you just couldn't wait to climb toward the impossible. I longed for you to believe that you were made to move mountains too.

And then, as they say, "life happened." It turns out when you set out to write a book about climbing mountains, there will be mountains to climb. When you dare to do the impossible, you will be faced with the impossible. When you stare fear in the face, life will scare you. I had no idea just how many personal challenges I would encounter in the process of writing this book. I guess that's how life is, isn't it? We never really know what's next. This book became its own daunting kind of mountain in my life. In writing the words on the pages that follow, I have been broken, hurt, angry, weary, relieved, afraid, fierce, unleashed. I started and stopped, scratched out words and began writing again and again, and have learned these anonymous words are true: "Writing is easy. You just open up a vein and bleed." By the time I began chapter 1, I faced a mountain I had not anticipated. Instead of feeling inspiring, I felt intimidated. Instead of feeling like a cheerleader, I felt like a coward. Instead of being your fearless trip leader, I was your weeping warrior. More than a glowing guide to climbing, this book became a very honest chronicle of how the inspiring mountain I'm on has also led me to the terrifying ones that loom in front of me.

There are smudges of my blood between the lines of this book. Some stories are incomplete because I'm still living them. But every word is a challenge for me—and you—to keep going.

I'm a mountain girl. Although I live much closer to the south beaches of Texas, I tolerate the sand but I love the mountains. There's just something peaceful about the gorgeous views, rolling heights, and crisp air. So as often as we can, my family heads to the mountains to enjoy long and challenging hikes, clocking hours and hours together in all kinds of terrain. And when we can't put our feet on them, we daydream about them.

When I long to get away, crave alone time with God, desire peace, I find it in higher altitudes. But mostly, I love the mountains because they heal me and simultaneously scare me half to death. They are very personal—not just because I love a good outdoor adventure but also because God has been writing an incredible story that has led me to the edge of the impossible. He hasn't just led me to the foot of the mountains. He's asked me to climb them, even though I'm afraid of heights. He's asked me to believe he is able to move them.

Over the past decade, I have watched God move mountains. The journey has been amazing, incredibly hard, and completely miraculous. But he didn't ask me to believe the impossible because there is something special or unique about me. I believe God allows or places the impossible in our paths so we can exercise our faith (and see it grow), and so he can show us how he makes the impossible possible. For me, one of those mountains was a difficult season in my marriage. In my memoir, *Rhinestone Jesus: Saying Yes to God When Sparkly Safe Faith Is No Longer Enough*, I wrote about how my marriage nearly fell apart at the ten-year mark when my husband confessed his addiction to pornography. But "something miraculous happened in the midst of our devastation."

The same night Terrell took a bold step and confessed his struggle to me was the same night I stepped toward him and started the process of forgiveness. Everything in me wanted to run away from this stranger I loved. But at the same time, I was so proud of him for wanting freedom more than he wanted to continue in the safety of his secret. We sobbed our way thru intimacy that night and even though we had never tasted so much brokenness, we knew that somehow God would redeem the ashes. We knew it would be the greatest battle of our lives—this choice to walk in freedom and forgiveness—but we decided in the middle of our devastation, we would fight for wholeness in our marriage.[1]

Scaling terrifying bluffs and dangling from high cliffs like these (metaphorically speaking, of course, because I'm not kidding about being scared of heights) has stretched my faith and grown my hope and confidence in Jesus more than anything else in my life.

It's my hope that the words in this book will challenge you to look at the mountains in your life a little differently—whether they are unwanted, like a diagnosis or a disaster, or a longed-for unfulfilled dream. We will take a closer look at what the Bible says about faith, trials, and how God is glorified in the difficult seasons. We will celebrate that God is always, always working on our behalf.

It seems that daily someone remarks about the path my family is on, and it is usually said with a bit of awe, as if we are different or somehow better or braver. I cringe every time I hear the words, and I remind them we are all made to move mountains. God created us to do hard things. We don't climb mountains because we're capable; we climb mountains because in our obedience, God is with us on the climb.

When Jon-Avery, my seventeen-year-old son, and I chatted about making a recording together on my podcast, *Mov-*

ing Mountains, he said something that stopped me in my tracks: "Mom, I want to remind people to look past their own mountains."

"What do you mean?" I asked.

"Well, it's easy to lose sight of the world's mountains when you're staring down your own. And we are always going to have obstacles in front of us and hard things to go through. That's life. But in caring about the mountains the rest of the world faces—big ones like poverty and bondage—our view changes. Our personal mountains don't look the same in the shadow of these mammoth ones."

Tears welled up in my eyes because what Jon-Avery was really talking about was justice. The theology of justice has rearranged my priorities and helped me to see past my own mountains, and I hope it does the same for you.

I thought of my life verse, Micah 6:8:

> He has shown you, O mortal, what is good.
>   And what does the LORD require of you?
> To act justly and to love mercy
>   and to walk humbly with your God.

This holy commission is why I'm on this mountain. Pursuing justice isn't only for lawyers and nonprofit leaders; it's a calling for every believer. Benjamin Franklin, one of our founding fathers, is widely thought to have said, "Justice will not be served until those who are unaffected are as outraged as those who are." Justice is caring about what Jesus cares about. What higher calling is there?

I hope this book will challenge you to pursue justice as a way of life and to see the obstacles you face a little differently. I pray you are inspired to step out in faith and climb the mountains in front of you—not because you are good enough or adequate or able, but because God makes a way where there seems to be no way.

We stand on the edge of the cliffs in our lives, and although we are afraid of stepping into the unknown, terrified where we will land and unsure of how to overcome, we do not run away. We stand firm in the face of the impossible, muster up as much faith as we can—even as small as a mustard seed—and we take one step.

We were made to move mountains.

1

The Mountain in Our Way

How do you move a mountain? One spoonful of
dirt at a time.

Chinese proverb

I'll never forget the first time I stood on the edge of a
mountain. I was a newlywed, and Terrell, my young
husband, and I were hiking. Even though he grew up near
Amarillo, Texas, which offers a flat terrain and a view for
miles, he was comfortable in the mountains because during
childhood family vacations he traipsed all kinds of rugged
terrain. I grew up on the other flat side of the state in a sub-
urb of Houston, and the only time my family had ever gone
camping ended with us loading up our tent in the rain and
heading home in the middle of the night. To say I wasn't in
my element on top of a mountain was an understatement.

If I had an element, it would have been called a safety net.
I have always loved my feet on the ground and adored my

comfort zone. I really liked what I knew. I wasn't a fan of change, and I didn't crave new and daring heights. I was an above-average control freak.

But still, the mountains called me. I think it was half wanting to please my new, outdoor-loving husband and the urge to explore Arkansas, the state we had just moved to. It probably also had something to do with our very limited salary and the fact that exploring the great outdoors was mostly free. We were youth pastors at a church near Little Rock, and when we needed to get away from the stress of ministry, we headed to the mountains. We had Mondays off, and we'd load up our Golden Retrievers and hike away our worries. The mountains became a place that meant rest and renewal (and sometimes escape) for the two of us.

On those early hikes, often I walked uphill behind my husband, stepping where he did until I became sure-footed. He would give me an encouraging tug or push along the way.

But I remember the first long hike we took. At the edge of my first mountain, I discovered a few things about myself. First, I was scared of heights. I was at the highest peak I had ever been to, and I didn't like it one bit. My fear didn't surprise me, but it did remind me that I liked control. The edge of the mountain terrified me. I stayed away from it—just to be safe. I had no desire to dangle my feet into the abyss below me. I wasn't a risk taker. Years later when I became a mom, my most-often-used parenting phrase to my children was "be careful." I still cringe at old home videos that recorded how many times I warned my family not to take risks.

The second thing I learned on the mountaintop was that my husband wasn't afraid at all. In theory, this wasn't a surprise either because I loved Terrell's adventurous side and his confidence to take new situations by storm. But loving him made me fear losing him. So when we climbed to the top and he immediately went to the edge to hang half his toes over, I flipped out. He called me over, and I refused. In the areas marked "danger," I watched in fear as he leaned over the railing and pushed every possible limit. The more fear I showed, the more he thrilled at the danger. Uh-oh. I had married a risk taker.

His thrill seeking and my comfort zone would clash in a million little ways as we learned to live together in the early years. We proved what they say about opposites attracting. I think it's safe to say that my voice of reason tempered some of his adventures and his risky behavior pushed me out of my comfort zone, and we found a place to meet in the middle. But even after twenty-five years of marriage, he still goes to the edge of every cliff while I beg him not to—some things never change. (If you read my book *Raising World Changers in a Changing World*, you know my middle-aged husband shattered his ankle on a skateboard. Point made.)

In the first decade of marriage, we climbed several mountains. We traded the Ozarks of Arkansas for the Jemez Mountains of New Mexico to become youth and children's pastors again. We strapped our babies into backpacks and climbed and climbed. We worked out a lot of challenges and struggles on those long hikes as a family.

We also faced mountains like financial stress and problems in our marriage. The church in Albuquerque that we called home for five years couldn't afford to pay us both, so for the first few years, we agreed to clean the church every week for extra money. We endured the mountain of infertility the first five years of our marriage as we dreamed of growing our family. After ten years of marriage, we left full-time ministry because we were burned out, and our marriage nearly fell apart. Challenging seasons in our lives teach us to overcome obstacles and face the giants on life's path. They also teach us endurance and courage.

In life's journey, I've learned there are mountains we climb because they challenge and inspire us and we long to see what's on the other side. Then there are mountains that show up in our paths we desperately want to move. Some mountains are dreams; others are disasters. We need grit and Jesus for both. Facing seeming impossibilities is a part of life—whether it's something we dream of doing or something we would never choose to climb. When we face a mountain, we are at a crossroads: we can either avoid it or climb it.

I love how author and artist Vera Nazarian gives us more choices: "If you are faced with a mountain, you have several options. You can climb it and cross to the other side. You can go around it. You can dig under it. You can fly over it. You can blow it up. You can ignore it and pretend it's not there. You can turn around and go back the way you came. Or you can stay on the mountain and make it your home."[1] No matter what we choose, we will all face mountains in our lives, *and I believe God wants us to climb them.*

Life is full of twists and turns, setbacks and successes. Every one of them will lead us back to Jesus if we let them. Whether we are on the mountaintop or in a low valley, God uses what we endure to draw us closer to him. Paul Washer, founder of HeartCry Missionary Society, puts it like this: "There are so many mountains in your life, so many obstacles in your life; so many things in your life that seek to derail you, to stop you. And they're going to stay there. Because some of those things don't just go away by counseling. They go away by falling on your face before God till He delivers you."[2]

For simplicity, I've put the mountains we face into two categories: dreams and disasters. Dreams are the mountains we don't have to climb but long to for some (often crazy) reason. Disasters are the mountains that we would never choose to climb.

Dreams

Whether it is an audacious dream to end global poverty or simply to open a bakery in your town because you make the best chocolate chip cookies and the world needs to taste them, dreams are, well, dreams. They may not always make sense to everyone else, but you imagine them coming true. I love this anonymous quote, "Every great dream begins with a dreamer. Always remember, you have within you the strength, the patience, and the passion to reach for the stars to change the world."

Years ago, when I really began dreaming, Terrell and I would go on coffee dates and "dreamstorm." I defined the term in my book *Rhinestone Jesus*:

Terrell and I curled up with a latte and did something we've never done before: we dreamstormed. "It's sort of like brainstorming," my husband said excitedly. "Except instead of writing down ideas, we're writing down our dreams. The wilder, bigger, and crazier, the better." We didn't hold back. Some of the things on our list included: working together again some day, starting a business so we could focus more on ministry and traveling internationally as a family.

Dreamstorming is a great exercise for your brain. Normally, our brains automatically zero in on all of the impossibilities we might face if we step out in faith and obedience. With dreamstorming, the impossible is replaced with the possible. It's amazing for my husband and I to look back at that list from years ago and see a few of the things coming to pass now. Let's face it: God likes to show off.

Your sweet spot isn't some elusive mystery that God dangles over your head, just beyond your grasp. It's the collision of believing in who you are and acting on it because of whom you belong to.[3]

So after more than a decade of dreaming of being a writer, I finally decided to become one. Saying yes was more about courage and faith than opportunity and success. I don't think we always recognize our God-sized dream for what it is, especially when it's wrapped up in our normalcy. I could identify with what writer Ann Voskamp said, "You were made for the place where your real passion meets compassion, because there lies your real purpose."[4]

I believe our sweet spot is also the place where our passion, our skills, and God's timing collide. In our sixteenth year of marriage with three kids and a middle-class income, we stood on the edge of the precipice of our lives. And we didn't just peer over the edge; we jumped. We didn't just dream of the impossible; we asked God for it.

In 2010, on my first trip to Kenya, I was exposed to global poverty, the third world's version of normal. I discovered that the third-world normal was vastly different from my own. My typical day included cooking and cleaning for my family, running errands, car line drop-offs and pickups, and maybe some Netflix. Seeing the world's normal for the first time helped me to understand that most of what I enjoyed (and often took for granted) wasn't typical for a mother living in a slum trying to figure out how to feed her family one meal a day.

This experience profoundly wrecked me. I returned home, and my new global perspective changed my everyday normal. I was tired of adjusting our lifestyle upward with every raise and extra dollar that came our way. While it gave us more stuff, it made us feel emptier. We decided we didn't want to change our lifestyle any longer—instead, we wanted to change lives. I couldn't shake the dream of doing something to empower oppressed and marginalized women in Kenya. We started Mercy House Global, an organization with a mission to engage, empower, and disciple women around the globe in Jesus's name. Talk about a mountain!

We didn't start Mercy House Global because we were brave or because we knew how to change the world. Honestly, we weren't that audacious. We were compelled to change the way we lived so that others could simply live. We were motivated to empower young leaders in Kenya. We stood on the edge of that mountain trembling, and we jumped because we believed God could do the impossible.

Over the last decade, we have watched God part the Red Sea, feed the five thousand, rain manna from heaven, shut the lion's mouth, and cast mountain after mountain into the sea. Mercy House Global has rescued more than fifty pregnant teen girls, and we've welcomed their miracle babies in the multiple maternity centers near Nairobi that our non-profit funds. We've empowered their families with dignified artisan jobs in an effort to break the generational poverty that imprisons so many. Mercy House Global works with over seventy artisan groups in more than thirty countries to replicate this goal by selling millions of dollars in fair-trade products every year—all to empower women around the globe in Jesus's name.

Dreams are hard. This one has broken me in ways I cannot explain. It has changed my family and given my kids a Mercy House childhood instead of one built on the American Dream. It's given them a global perspective, but it's also required enormous sacrifices. It's made me desperate for Jesus. In some ways, it has cost our family. But it's turned me into a hard worker. Retired four-star General Colin Powell said, "A dream doesn't become reality through magic; it takes sweat, determination and hard work."[5]

Most days, I'm still that scared girl at the edge of the cliff scrambling for control, feeling overwhelmed and inadequate in every way. Our family offered what we had—our small lunch of fish and loaves. It certainly wasn't enough to meet the need, but Jesus took it and made it perfect in our weakness. So, no, we haven't moved mountains by ourselves; we have stood on holy ground and watched God cast them into the sea. We have been eyewitnesses to the miraculous. We scrounged every bit of faith we could muster and unleashed it in the face of the impossible because, as A. W. Tozer said, we believe that's the kind of people God is looking for: "God is looking for those with whom he can do the impossible—what a pity that we plan only the things that we can do by ourselves."[6]

You may be thinking, *There's no way I could ever climb a mountain that high.* I know exactly what you mean because I felt the same way. And we can't; only God can. That first step, our small "yes Lord," can lead us to places we never thought possible. Even in my wildest dreams of helping pregnant teens in Kenya, I didn't dream of more than fifty. I didn't imagine we would provide jobs for their families or that fair-trade products would be the vehicle to do it. That's what is so incredible about dreaming with God. We have a small idea of what we can do, but we have no idea what he can do with our willingness! Let's call out the elephant on the page: you were made to move mountains. We all were, not just a select few.

One of the things I've hated about this journey is the assumption that people who go after their mountains or accomplish what the world would call "big dreams" are special, unique, gifted, or rare. You were created, designed, and purposed to move mountains too. It's in your DNA; it's your destiny.

I sat in the office of a large church in Texas, trying to explain how Mercy House began. We had been invited to present our ministry because the church had money to give away at the end of the year, and they were considering making a big donation to our nonprofit. It was a one-of-a-kind offer that isn't part of our normal. For the briefest moment, I didn't know how to begin. I knew my job was to convince them that we were worthy of their money, but all I could think was *I'm not supposed to be here.* As I sat there on a bright yellow chair, wringing my hands, I tried to find a place to start the story of the last decade that has turned my life rightside up. I decided to begin with the truth: "I'm not supposed to be here. I'm a mom, a writer, a person who is forever behind on laundry." But I told them through tears how God used the poor to show me my own poverty. How—against all odds—we opened maternity homes in Kenya, have welcomed dozens of pregnant teen survivors, started Fair Trade Friday to provide dignified jobs in Jesus's name, and opened retail stores at which we sell a lot of fair-trade products.

I told them that I have panic attacks on nearly every overseas trip I take, that I had recently endured burnout and wound up on a counselor's couch, that I carry the trauma of fifty girls' horrific stories, that I have asked my family to give and give and give some more, and that I have some amazing days but mostly I feel overwhelmed, tired, and very alone. I told them that this yes to God has cost me some of the most precious relationships in my life. I told them that often I want to quit. I took a deep breath and ended my "presentation" with "I have no idea why God asked me to do this." So, yeah, I nailed it. It was just another example of how inadequate I felt for this job. I didn't have a slideshow, a business plan, or even note cards. I had compelling stories and tears, lots of tears.

After I dumped my heart on the table between us, the room was deathly quiet. And then the missions pastor leaned across the table and said something that I promise is holy and prophetic and exactly what I need to tell myself every single day: "Kristen, God likes bad odds."

His words reminded me of what Louie Giglio, pastor of Passion City Church, said, "Whatever giant we're battling might be big—but it's not bigger than Jesus."[7] I pulled out a pen and right there in that church office, I wrote his words big and bold across my paper. *God likes bad odds.* He isn't a gambler; he isn't taking a risk on us. He is confident in his strength in our weakness. God uses flawed people to reach a flawed world. We are in good company, friends.

Pastor and author Jarrid Wilson listed the following: Abraham was old. Elijah was suicidal. Joseph was abused.

Job went bankrupt. Moses had a speech problem. Gideon was afraid. Samson was a womanizer. Rahab was a prostitute. The Samaritan woman was divorced (five times). Noah was a drunk. Jeremiah was young. Jacob was a cheater. David was a murderer. Jonah ran from God. Naomi was a widow. Peter denied Christ three times. Martha worried about everything. Zacchaeus was small and money hungry. The disciples fell asleep while praying. Paul was a Pharisee who persecuted Christians before becoming one.[8]

Believe me, God isn't asking us at Mercy House Global to do something we know how to do. He isn't counting on our expertise or perfection. He is betting on our inadequacies and weaknesses. He knows the odds, and the cards are stacked against us. I have no idea how we will continue to empower women globally. It's enough to make me cry and beg and worry because I don't know how to do this. Remember, I don't even know how to get all my laundry done. But I think it's okay because I'm not supposed to know the how—I know the Who.

Unfortunately, there are other mountains that show up in our lives that we would never choose. They aren't dreams or longings. They are life-and-death obstacles that require every ounce of strength and determination we can muster.

Disasters

I've lived in some disaster zones in my lifetime. Disasters change us. They scare us and remind us of life's uncertainty and unpredictability. They force us to either flounder on our own understanding or find Jesus in the aftermath. While I was visiting my parents on a college break, a devastating tornado hit their Dallas suburban home and nearly destroyed it. I will never forget the destructive wind that drove us to our faces as we belly crawled through the house in the dark in the middle of the night looking for one another. As long as I live, I will never forget my parents lying on top of me in protection from the flying debris swirling around us. The storm killed a neighbor and destroyed our neighborhood. It was terrifying. We lived in a disaster zone for months afterward while the Red Cross delivered food to those who were cleaning up and rebuilding. We shopped for clothes to wear at the local high school gym where people had donated needed items. It was humbling and hard.

Other storms and hurricanes have blown my way. In 2017, my family endured Hurricane Harvey. We helplessly watched the floodwaters rise for days in our hometown of Houston and spent the weeks afterward mucking out houses of friends and strangers with crews from our church. We turned our nonprofit into a relief area where we collected items for storm victims. We witnessed the beautiful community that often arises following a storm. We celebrated with friends as they rebuilt their lives and homes.

I've had other seasons of devastation in my life as well. We don't ask for disasters in our lives. Well, generally, *I don't*. One time, my young husband stood on the front porch because the tornado sirens were going off and he wanted to see if he could spot one. I was in the fetal position in the empty bathtub with a mattress over my head, screaming, "You're going to die!" We don't seek out disease, death, despair, or depression. But trials come anyway.

In my case, I feel as if many of my dreams have led to some of the biggest disasters in my life. I'll explain more as we go, but one thing I know with certainty is that dreams and disasters make room for the divine. I don't know what kind of mountain you are facing today—an enormous dream, an impossible disaster, or maybe a dose of both. But I do know that our motivation for wanting the mountains moved matters. If we want God to do the impossible so that he will be glorified, we are standing on ground that can be moved.

We also must remember that if Jesus doesn't move the mountain or perform the miracle, he is still good. We praise him when he does the impossible, and we praise him when he does not. We are really talking about faith in action. Hebrews 11:1 says, "Now faith is confidence in what we hope for and assurance about what we do not see." We long for the impossible not because we deserve it. We hope for it because when God moves mountains, he is glorified in and through our dreams and disasters. Faith is the foundation of the Christian life and the means by which all unseen things are tested. Faith means we trust in what God has promised, resulting in a life of faithfulness and perseverance.

David Brooks, a *New York Times* writer and author, offers a stunning image in his book *The Second Mountain*. It shows two mountains next to each other. The first is composed of multiple uses of the word *me* piled on top of one another. The second mountain is composed of many more uses of the word *us* piled higher than the first mountain. He describes first-mountain people as divided and alienated and their culture as insufficient. They suffer from "a rot" in their "moral and cultural foundations."[9] Second-mountain people, having given themselves away, lead lives of deep commitment. For them, happiness is good but joy is better. "Happiness comes from accomplishments; joy comes from offering gifts.

33

Happiness fades; we get used to the things that used to make us happy. Joy doesn't fade. To live with joy is to live with wonder, gratitude, and hope. People who are on the second mountain have been transformed. They are deeply committed. The outpouring of love has become a steady force."[10]

Both kinds of mountain people have problems and face challenges. But being second-mountain "us" people helps us overcome the "me" mountains.

Brooks says that self-satisfaction is the primary goal of first-mountain people while second mountaineers radiate gratitude, delight, and kindness.

Friends, let's take a minute to stop and reflect. I mean truly stop what you're doing—earmark the page, turn this book over—and think about your life and the path you are on. What kind of mountain are you climbing? Are you at a crossroads? What is the view behind you, and what does the road ahead look like?

Likely, there's a mountain or two in sight. What kind of mountain are you facing? Is it a crazy, afraid-to-say-it-aloud, God-sized dream? If so, define it. Say it out loud.

Or are you staring down an uncertain, scary obstacle that showed up on your path and you don't even know where to begin?

Maybe you are like me, and right now, today, it's both: a beautiful journey I want to take and a broken one that I don't. While they are certainly different challenges, I'm taking the same approach to both kinds of impossibilities. I'm starting with my heart.

Proverbs 23:7 says, "For as he thinks in his heart, so is he" (NKJV). Long before we take a first step, we make a decision in our hearts. It's the birthplace of dreams and determination. God sees our motives long before we confess them, but I think it's critical to examine our motivation for climbing. Do we long to see mountains moved for our own glory, recognition, and success, or do we desire the impossible because it will glorify God?

MOUNTAINTOP MOMENT

Let's take a deeper look into what our motivation is for desiring mountains moved in our lives. Whether they are something we dream of doing or dread facing, let's start here.

1. Read Acts 5:12–20.
2. We see the miracle in these verses. God sent an angel to open the door so that people could hear the good news. God moves mountains for a reason. Reflect on your mountain and your motivation for moving it.
3. Throughout the Old Testament, God encouraged his people to set up memorial stones as remembrances. It takes a lot of courage to put something in writing. It's often the first big step—to record it even if it's for your eyes only. If you're ready, write down your dream or disaster or just a word that is between you and God. (I did this in a private prayer journal, and recently, when I reread my words, I couldn't believe that many of the dreams were now reality.)

Journal

2

Rejoicing in the Impossible

> There are many paths up the mountain, but the
> view from the top is always the same.
>
> Chinese proverb

*T*his is what I've learned. God moves some mountains miraculously. We stare down the impossible, and it stares right back at us. But then God casts it into the sea and makes a way where there wasn't one. And some mountains God does not move. They are out in front of us—blocking our paths, obscuring our views, wearing us out. These mountains were created for us to climb.

Many days we face obstacles that weren't there the day before—and suddenly they are threatening us: a diagnosis, a disaster, discouraging news, depression, or despair. I've dug my feet into a few of these mountains this year, and I've spent a lot of time telling God about the mountains in front of me. Maybe you have too.

A couple of years ago, my family drove the eighteen long hours to Colorado until we got to the mountains my husband climbed as a boy. We were looking for a certain spot he and his father visited nearly forty years ago where they had built a small rock memorial and hidden some coins. There was no reason behind it other than a dad and his son on an adventure, creating a memory. Terrell had told our kids the story about this little memorial for years, and he always wondered if it was still there. Terrell's parents met us in Colorado, and together, they narrowed down the area with a fuzzy memory. Then, we climbed.

And we climbed some more—huffing and puffing and panting our way to the top. We were discouraged when we couldn't find any trace of it. Everyone was disappointed, but a lot changes in forty years! We found a good spot and built our own pile of rocks so that our kids could bring their children to hunt for it maybe forty years from now. We had learned that building memories and remembering them is half the journey. As we stood on the top of that mountain in the crisp air, I turned to look behind us. I was surprised at how high we had climbed.

It's a lot easier to see the top of one mountain from another. Some days, we need to look behind us to see how many mountains we've already scaled. It's too easy to forget that much of what we enjoy today is what we asked God for yesterday. When we reflect on what God has already done in our lives, our hearts, and our homes and we stop and praise him for it—our perspective changes everything.

The God who led us to the foot of the mountain is the same God who will lead us over it. Instead of telling God about the big mountain in front of us, let's tell the mountain about our big God. In *Raising World Changers in a Changing World*, I wrote about one of the trips my family took to Kenya that exposed us to the world's normal and altered our normal forever.

> We entered a home that was smaller than our master bathroom and squinted in the dark to find a place to sit. When our eyes adjusted to the light we cringed as bedbugs crawled all over us.
>
> I couldn't believe seven people lived in this stifling, dark room. The heat wasn't as oppressive as the lack of hope. I slid my camera back into my bag because I knew there would be no pictures here. There weren't any smiling faces or laughing children. There was a heaviness in the air I can't explain.
>
> The home belonged to the mother of one of the teen moms from the maternity home, and our staff in Kenya wanted us to understand why we needed a transition home for some of the girls and their children. And they needed us to know why providing jobs is so critical.
>
> When we asked how we could pray for her, she shared about the difficult issues in her marriage and the abuse by her drunken husband. We held hands and prayed over her. It was hot and hard to shake the hopelessness that pervaded the room. Just as we were preparing to leave, her husband walked in the door—drunk.
>
> And just like that, my little family was in the middle of a heated dispute in a dangerous slum with angry words being flung back and forth in Swahili. We sat back down. I held my little girl's hand and whispered a prayer for peace and safety as we sat there, unsure of what was being said. I won't lie—in that half hour I didn't feel brave at all and longed to return to my normal.
>
> But as soon as I thought it, I heard the words thunder in my heart: *This is their normal.*[1]

Our family left the slum that day with our Kenyan directors and found the nearest public restroom at a restaurant to shake the bedbugs out of our clothes. Over a burger and fries, we brainstormed possible solutions to create dignified jobs for the precious, illiterate mothers of the teen moms in our maternity homes. We settled on textiles and ceramics. It felt like another huge step in this journey since we knew nothing about either. But we wanted to keep an indigenous trade alive, it was a low start-up cost, and God had opened doors by providing Kenyan teachers for both.

When we returned to America, we again asked God to do the impossible for the grandmothers of the nineteen babies whose moms could not transition home because of the extreme poverty and suffering their families lived in. I read Matthew 21:21 over and over, "Truly I tell you, if you have faith and do not doubt, not only can you do what was done to the fig tree, but also you can say to this mountain, 'Go, throw yourself into the sea,' and it will be done."

We bought looms and kilns, and we stared down a mountain of impossibilities as we worked to turn very poor, uneducated women into skilled artisans. I asked my daughter Madison to watercolor a mountain logo for our newest artisan group we called Miujiza, which means *miracles* in Swahili. I felt nearly as desperate to provide work as the women were to find jobs. I watched and waited and tried to keep my head up—to just keep going. And I worried. Would the women be able to learn this difficult skill? Would we be able to sell rugs? Would this even work? I doubted. I was afraid. The moment you are ready to quit is usually the moment right before the miracle occurs. Faith produces hope.

It was time to return to Kenya and stand at the looms and sit in the homes and report on this miracle project. But every time I leave my family and get on a plane to fly across the ocean, it is difficult for me. My mental countdown to Go-day is pathetic. It just doesn't get easier for me to go. I don't mean to sound spoiled or ungrateful; please don't get me wrong. I love being sent. I love that Jesus expects obedience even when we'd rather stay put.

A friend visiting me at work at Mercy House asked if she could pray with me before I left for Kenya. I could hardly respond yes fast enough. I asked the staff nearby to gather around, and we prayed. As we finished, one of my staff members let out a "Whoop! Yay! You're going on an adventure!" I gave a weak smile. I like staying. But when we go—even in fear and doubt and with a dab of dread—we let go of control. We remind ourselves God is in charge. We may be uncomfortable, but in this dynamic, we remember the beauty of saying yes. Behind every fear, a miracle is waiting.

Back in Kenya, I walked into a room with nine grand-mothers—some of whom had sold their own girls into slavery and others who had watched helplessly as their daughters were abused—and I witnessed *miujiza*, miracles. I've sat in every one of their homes in slums across Nairobi and wept at their hopeless situations. But as I watched these master weavers turn strands of thread into gorgeous textiles, I knew this was holy ground. Madison was with me, and I squeezed her hand and reminded her of the mountains she painted.

After visiting the jaw-dropping beauty of our women—the most unlikely of weavers—sitting at looms creating masterpieces, we stopped for lunch at a nearby market. The weight of the world should have been lifted—it was working, the women were weaving!

But I tend to pick up where I left off, and as I drank Coca-Cola from a bottle, I fretted about the next stage, selling the rugs. It takes five days to weave one rug, and the materials made in Kenya aren't cheap. Once we added in the cost of paying the women, I realized our rugs were going to be expensive. Most handmade things are, but we live in a culture that values bargains and doesn't always consider the hands behind the product. We've made it a mission at Mercy House Global to educate consumers to consider where the products they buy are made. When we can purchase something that not only provides a decent wage but also freedom, why wouldn't we?

Becky, a friend who has been wildly generous to Mercy House, was on the trip with me, and she wasn't at all worried about our ability to sell the rugs. I wondered at her positive attitude, and she put her burger down, leaned toward me, and with tears in her eyes said, "I need to tell you my rug story." I stopped eating because I needed to hear it.

"Three years ago, I had never heard of Mercy House Global. I had just finished reading the Bible through for the first time, and I saw one constant theme throughout: you cannot give God more than he will give you. I was in Colorado on a girls' weekend trip when I walked into a high-end boutique and saw a gorgeous rug that would be perfect for my living room. I had been searching for something exactly like it, but it had a huge price tag. I wavered, debating if I should spend thousands of dollars. I left the boutique and then returned to it because I couldn't stop thinking about that rug. As I stood there, I felt as if God spoke to me. He said, 'Don't buy this rug. Hold on to that money, and I'll tell you where to give it. You will have your choice of rugs.'" She admitted she had no idea what the message meant, but it had been impressed upon her that this wasn't about money; it was about obedience. She didn't understand it, but she knew the right rug would find her.

Three weeks later, Becky was invited to the Mercy House Gala at which I told the story of Miujiza and we auctioned off the first rug from our looms in Kenya. "Kristen, that night, God said to me, 'This is where you're supposed to give that money.' I bid on the first rug, and today I witnessed gorgeous rugs being made. So see? I'm not worried about Mercy House selling rugs at all."

I cried all over my burger. Three years ago, God was talking about rugs to someone I had never met and before I knew we would even be making them. Why? Because God sees us. He knows where we are and what we are doing. He pursues us. He prepares. He puts people in our paths. He pushes us out of our comfort zones and puts us in places where we can hear him. We see this throughout the Bible.

For more than two years now, my pastor has been teaching our church verse by verse through the book of Acts. As we read about Saul's conversion in Acts 9, I understood it in a new way. Saul became Paul because God interrupted his life. He put Saul in a hard place where he was forced to listen.

In Damascus there was a disciple named Ananias. The Lord called to him in a vision, "Ananias!"

"Yes, Lord," he answered.

The Lord told him, "Go to the house of Judas on Straight Street and ask for a man from Tarsus named Saul, for he is praying. In a vision he has seen a man named Ananias come and place his hands on him to restore his sight."

"Lord," Ananias answered, "I have heard many reports about this man and all the harm he has done to your holy people in Jerusalem. And he has come here with authority from the chief priests to arrest all who call on your name."

But the Lord said to Ananias, "Go! This man is my chosen instrument to proclaim my name to the Gentiles and their kings and to the people of Israel. I will show him how much he must suffer for my name."

Then Ananias went to the house and entered it. Placing his hands on Saul, he said, "Brother Saul, the Lord—Jesus, who appeared to you on the road as you were coming here—has sent me so that you may see again and be filled with the Holy Spirit." Immediately, something like scales fell from Saul's eyes, and he could see again. He got up and was baptized, and after taking some food, he regained his strength. (vv. 10–19)

As Saul sat and waited, blinded by scales over his eyes, God was about to do the impossible—turn a vicious murderer of Christians into a victorious follower of Christ.

I have read the story many times, but for the first time I understood how difficult it must have been—how impossible it must have felt—for Ananias to go. God spoke to Ananias and told him to find Saul. Ananias was afraid to do what God asked of him. Can you imagine how terrified he likely was?

Today, it might be comparable to approaching an ISIS leader and asking to pray for him. But God does not let our fear stop us from doing what he asks us to do. He didn't change the plan because Ananias was afraid. God does not submit to our fears; he is not concerned about our discomfort. He understands and says to go anyway. He calls us to a life that matters. When we go, he goes with us.

I believe God can do the impossible without us. He is God, after all; he can do anything. But he often invites us into the miracle. He allows us to be a part of it so that our faith will increase, so that people will see the impossible made possible, and above all, so that he will be glorified. I have wondered how often my refusal to obey, my hesitancy to go, or my action altered by my fear has kept the impossible *impossible*. How many opportunities have I missed to witness the miraculous because I didn't listen or wouldn't obey? *God, remove the scales from our eyes so that we may see you clearly.*

MOUNTAINTOP MOMENT

God created us with a sense of adventure. But in our culture, we are addicted to comfort and safety. We live vicariously through reality TV and take part in adventure via video games. We are tempted to sit back and simply watch life happening around us. We may wish we were brave enough, strong enough to step into the unknown.

In *Reckless Faith*, Kevin Harney challenges readers to believe that God didn't create us to live safe lives. "Reckless faith is a God-ordained leap of faithfulness inspired by the Holy Spirit and consistent with Scripture." [2] A dream might be driving you to the edge of a mountaintop, or a disaster might not have given you a choice. Either way, today, you are at a crossroads.

You were meant to move the mountain in front of you. God is calling you to unleash your faith in the face of your impossible and believe for a miracle. Author O. R. Melling wrote, "When you come to the edge of all that you know, you must believe one of two things: either there will be ground to stand on, or you will be given wings to fly." [3]

1. Read Hebrews 11.
2. Study the Bible's definition of faith: confidence and assurance.
3. How can you actively obey? Write down a couple of tangible responses of active faith.

3

The Best View Means
the Hardest Climb

By trials God is shaping us for higher things.

Jeremy Taylor

Mom, you've been talking a lot about climbing mountains lately. You're writing a whole book about it.
Maybe you should actually climb one?"

Everyone laughed at Emerson's challenge, including me—
nervously. Let's just say I'm not the athlete in the family. I
could hear the teasing in my youngest daughter's words,
but mostly I heard the dare to do more than walk up hills.

She reminded me of her big sister, Madison, who at the
time was between high school graduation and college. She
was still our child but also a budding adult. There was a
new tension between us as she prepared to leave home. We
both knew it would never be the same. Honestly, I thought
that summer would be filled with beautiful, meaningful

memories, but instead there was a lot of arguing and pushing against each other.

I texted a desperate question to a friend who had already launched three strong-willed daughters into college and adulthood: "Is this normal?!"

She reassured me that the last summer home is hard and good and, well, there's a reason you are ready for them to leave the nest when they finally do. "Yes, it's normal."

I wept at her words that made me feel better about my expectations for a "perfect" last summer together. So when my kids challenged me to find a cliff, I appeased them by signing up our family for a 5K. They were shocked and excited! They giggled when I downloaded the Couch to 5K app, but when I crossed the finish line totally out of breath, they were there waiting for me to put the medal around my neck. (I didn't make them run at my pace.) They understood that for me this race wasn't about setting records; it was about finishing. It was also about accepting their challenge to do something physically demanding. We've run two more since! Of course, I found it ironic that they didn't realize how often parenting felt like climbing a mammoth mountain rather than completing a community race.

If you are a parent, you know exactly what I mean. Every stage and phase presents unique challenges that we usually aren't ready for and that can drive us to our knees. Ask a mom who hasn't had a full night's sleep in a year or one who is standing toe-to-toe with a strong-willed child. The parent-child relationship is a paradox like no other because some of our best, most profound mountaintop experiences are with our kids.

Let me step in mom-to-mom or parent-to-parent and give you a tiny bit of advice. I might not be ahead of you on this journey, but I did successfully launch one kid and the next one is stretching his wings. I shared the following on my blog in January 2019:

> I got stuck in a shirt in a dressing room at a local thrift shop, and with my arms up in the air, I actually thought about buying the dumb top because that seemed easier than escaping it. As I wriggled my way out of it, I reminded my middle-aged self that not all size mediums are created equal.
>
> I used to believe that not all moms were created equal too. I wasn't like the other moms who had it all together. I showed up at bake sales with store-bought treats and I was always the mom who was on her phone trying to solve a crisis overseas. I never felt present enough and struggled with guilt as a working mom.
>
> I finally accepted that the way I mother is the way I mother and there is not an equation that makes one mom unequal to another.
>
> Now, every time I see a young mother wrestling her kids into their car seats or juggling toddlers and a baby and a week's worth of groceries, I'm grateful I'm past that season. At least until I tell my teens they need to do their laundry, ground them, or remind them to clean their rooms and then I really miss nap time. And cribs.
>
> With one off at college and another starting to talk about what colleges he's interested in, this season of life is strange. It's hard in a different kind of way. It's less physical and more emotional. When my girl calls me from college—I stop everything. Everything. I stalk her on social media and keep friending her college buddies. (I'm sorry, honey.)
>
> The other day, my college freshman was in town for just an hour on a Sunday morning. She texted "Want to grab a quick lunch before I have to leave again?" We turned

the car away from church and drove nearly half an hour so we could all eat tacos together. I quickly snapped this picture of my three beautiful babies in the booth together. On some hard days lately, each going through their own challenges, I have whispered to myself, to them, you are going to be okay.

Awhile back, my husband was cleaning out his sock drawer and found an old kindergarten picture of our son. I smiled at the memory of him in the red, white and blue collared polo shirt. I turned it over to read the date. It was taken ten years ago. My son grabbed it and said, "Mom, you dressed me like a dork."

Yes, yes I did.

I thought back to the mom I was fifteen years ago and one word came to mind: high-strung. I worried constantly about everything. Sure, I had firmer arms and thought my 30s were way better than my 20s, but I was overprotective and over-reactive and overbearing—then my 40s happened and I got over it. If I could say anything to my mom-self fifteen years ago, it would be to calm down. Take motherhood down a notch. Your kids are going to be okay.

It won't be perfect and neither will you. But they will be okay.

The messy rooms and dirty floors, the store-bought cook-ies, the red ribbon weeks we ignored, the broken screen-time rules, the mediocre dinners, the okay preschools, the hand-me-downs and homework folders we didn't sign, the curriculum we chose, the colleges they choose, the broken hearts we can't mend—all these things we lose sleep over—they won't ruin our kids.

When we forget picture day and tooth fairy duties and the spelling test, when we are late for car line again or can't find the poop smell in the house or the missing hamster, when we make them wear too-small shoes one more day, when we say no, when we let our kids down—they will survive.

Often their disappointment and failure, sadness and anger isn't ruining them. It's growing them up. And, it's maturing you too. You're learning how to let go of what doesn't really matter. They will be okay. You want to know why? Because we keep showing up. It turns out, that's exactly what our kids need most. Moms that are there. Period. My sixteen-year-old son doesn't need me to solve his problems—he just wants me to walk with him through them. My tween doesn't need me to be everything, she just needs me to be present.

So, Momma, take a deep breath and let it out. Let it go. You are doing just fine. Your kids are going to be okay.[1]

When we are facing down a giant mountain, it's often all we can see. It fills our vision and our senses, and it overpowers our thoughts. Mountains can consume us and can often skew our perspective. It's easy to lose our outlook because we can't see past what's in front of us.

I started this book while our family was on a sabbatical in a tiny New Mexican mountain town for the same reason. We needed a new perspective.

The board of directors at Mercy House Global urged our family to take a month off after nearly a decade of dreaming and doing. It's difficult not to let the work we do consume our family. Our home is behind one of our retail stores, and our church houses the other. It's very hard to get away from work even when we are at home. Because Terrell and I both work full-time at Mercy House, the line between family and work and ministry is often blurry. We saw the wisdom in their leadership and planned a trip to the mountains. I knew that if we were truly going to take the break we needed, we had to leave town.

I learned quickly how tough it is (and how much work is required) to leave your life behind for a month. Honestly, by the time we pointed our van toward the mountains, we were exhausted, completely weary. It took two weeks for me to truly feel relaxed, but even rest in the mountains brings its own challenges. The rest and relaxation that Terrell and I so desperately needed became a challenge for our children. (Read: they were mostly bored out of their minds.)

Isn't that just how life is? If we aren't going through a trial, someone we love is. And we don't get to decide whose mountain is easier to overcome. Some challenges I face are dreams for others. Some disasters you face are nothing in comparison to what others experience. That's why I love this anonymous quote I've seen floating around Pinterest: "You have been assigned this mountain to show others that it can be moved."

It took me five long years to get pregnant with Madison. I never dreamed infertility would be a challenge in my journey. Six years later, I had a miscarriage and the year after that, a premature baby—every experience was hard and heartbreaking. But now that those experiences are in my rearview mirror, I have used them to empathize with and encourage others. I don't know why I experienced those and many other trials, but I do think the reasons I endured infertility and a premature baby, struggles and defeat in church ministry, financial difficulties, and the breakdown of my marriage (all of which I wrote about in *Rhinestone Jesus*) were so that I could mature, empathize with others, and glorify God. After traveling to Kenya in 2010, I experienced a complete midlife overhaul and transformation when I woke up from the American Dream, stopped living an entitled, selfish life, and began pursuing justice for others rather than enjoying it only for myself. These were desperately lonely and difficult seasons in which I met Jesus face-to-face. These times helped me not only face whatever was in my path but also draw strength from knowing I wasn't alone.

God gives us opportunities to encourage others who face the same mountains we do. Paul writes:

> He comforts us in all our troubles so that we can comfort others. When they are troubled, we will be able to give them the same comfort God has given us. For the more we suffer for Christ, the more God will shower us with his comfort through Christ. Even when we are weighed down with troubles, it is for your comfort and salvation! For when we ourselves are comforted, we will certainly comfort you. Then you can patiently endure the same things we suffer. (2 Cor. 1:4–6 NLT)

Perspective is everything. Two people can look at the exact same problem: one can feel inspired and the other can feel overwhelmed. That is why it's great to change places when we can or to put ourselves in another person's shoes—the problem doesn't change, but the way we see it does. We see either opportunities or obstacles.

Almost anything can be a mountain in our lives—difficult phases of parenting, challenges in our marriages, dreams and disasters, a boring month in the mountains, even writing books about moving them. As believers, we are promised trials and tests of our faith. It's not a matter of if; it's a matter of when. But we find promise and hope and even direction in James 1:2–4: "Consider it pure joy, my brothers and sisters, whenever you face trials of many kinds, because you know that the testing of your faith produces perseverance. Let perseverance finish its work so that you may be mature and complete, not lacking anything."

Why does God allow trials in our lives? It's a universal question and has been asked for ages. If God is powerful and good, why doesn't he stop our pain and suffering? I don't pretend to be smart or wise enough to answer a question that has perplexed and plagued generations. But I do believe the ultimate reason God allows trials in our lives is because they develop character in us. They push us to persevere, increasing our faith and restoring our hope. Our mountains glorify our heavenly Father.

Character

Not many people know about a very personal and painful season in my life. I've never written about it because of the impact my story has on other people I know and love. Without sharing too many details, I will say I've had to establish healthy boundaries and extend as much grace as possible in some of my relationships. I haven't always gotten this balance right, and it has been a continual challenge to trust Jesus with my heart.

When God dropped the title of this book in my lap, I was completely convinced it was the direction I was looking for, and I was excited about its message. But just days after my publisher agreed that this would be my next book, my heart was broken by people I love. I couldn't eat or sleep. I was confused and hurt, angry and tired. But even in the pain, I knew God's timing was significant.

He had just allowed an enormous mountain to stop me in my tracks.

I remember crying out to God and pointing out the irony of what I wanted to write about in regard to what I was now facing. How could I encourage people to overcome what they were going through when I was facing something so impossible? The enemy taunted me with the ugly words and lies that had been hurled my way. At the time, I couldn't imagine reconciliation. Months passed, and I didn't write a word of the manuscript. I couldn't. I didn't have an ounce of faith for the miracle I needed. I was defeated. But defeat isn't the end, according to Henry Ward Beecher: "It is defeat that turns bone to flint, gristle to muscle, and makes men invincible. One is never so near victory as when defeated in a good cause."[2]

I don't know why we go through difficult seasons like these, but I am proof they make us stronger. During that time, I reminded myself constantly that hurting people hurt people, but healed people heal people. I continued to offer this mountain to God even when I still couldn't see any way around it. I constantly prayed and asked God to help me walk in love and forgiveness. Francis Chan's words challenged me: "God doesn't call us to be comfortable. He calls us to trust Him so completely that we are unafraid to put ourselves in situations where we will be in trouble if He doesn't come through."[3]

I was reminded that sometimes the right thing is also the hardest thing. John Eldredge says in *Moving Mountains*, "Sometimes it takes time for a person to be ready to forgive. It often helps to explain that forgiveness is not saying it didn't matter; it is not saying we simply choose to overlook the offense. Forgiveness is saying the cross is enough—we require no further payment than Jesus paid. Forgiveness is releasing the person to God for him to deal with."[4]

I'm still trying to navigate my way through challenging personal relationships, but I'm not sorry I'm on this mountain. I'm climbing my way over it, one step at a time. God refines us in the fire because he wants us to grow into mature Christians. God told the children of Israel that he put them in the fire so that he may "refine them as one refines silver, and test them as gold is tested" (Zech. 13:9 ESV).

On one of my trips to Kenya, I stood at an extremely hot furnace and watched as artisans placed pieces and spare metal parts into the fire. The heat was nearly unbearable as the metals melted into hot molten liquid. It was then poured into jewelry molds, and something entirely new was made. The heat of the fire created something new. When we face fiery trials we don't deserve and don't understand, we must believe that God is forging something new and good in us. He's burning away what is impure. It can be painful, but we aren't alone in the fire.

Perseverance

I love this quote by author and Simple Way founder Shane Claiborne: "When we ask God to move a mountain, God may give us a shovel."[5] When we returned from our sabbatical, we returned to a load of work. Isn't that always how it is? You plan a vacation or time away and work hard to make it happen so you can rest. But when you return, you find the work didn't stop, and you have to dig yourself out. After a couple of days back in the office, we realized we had a serious cash-flow problem.

At any given time, Mercy House has more than a quarter million dollars out in paid invoices to artisan groups around the world for our fair-trade subscription clubs, which are planned six months to a year in advance. We create a concept for a themed box, ask artisans to fulfill the order, and pay them at least 50 percent down and often the full invoice to do so. Mercy House carries the burden instead of placing it on smaller groups. The products are presold through our clubs, but we don't receive payment until a week or two before the items ship. The combination of that component, slower summer months, and a drop-off in membership, and we had a minicrisis that was growing daily. You could call it a mountain, and I wanted to head for the hills.

I've had some dark days on this mountain-moving journey, but this was one of the lowest points for me. Not because I didn't believe God would provide again, but because I knew this was our lives—constantly needing miracles and mountains moved. After a month off, I was physically renewed, but this unexpected emergency was beyond discouraging. I won't lie and say I haven't thought about quitting many times, but this was the first time I wanted to quit. I imagined walking away. I dreamed of giving up. I wrote these words on my blog on July 23, 2018, one week after returning from our sabbatical:

Friends,

One year ago today, I was in Kenya with some of our staff. We stood in the city dump that is simply indescribable. We watched women and young girls, covered in filth and living in a hellhole, dig for food and search for items to sell. Most make less than twenty-five cents a day in their quest.

It was just another day at work for them. I had to cover my mouth with a scarf to keep from vomiting. Pictures and words do not do this place justice. Our Kenyan director leaned over and whispered in my ear, remember this place when you want to quit. You will never quit as long as you know that there are women so desperate for work they make this their job.

I remember thinking, overwhelmed with the view and the desperation, maybe even with pride, "Oh, I will never want to quit after this."

But today, when I woke up, that's exactly what I wanted to do.

I don't think it's an accident that on the day when I most wanted to quit, God sent a very clear reminder with some Facebook memories that urged me not to give up but instead give it all to Him. I cannot quit as long as women dig in dumps to feed their kids.

It's with a heavy heart that I write to you today. Some of you are personal friends, others are shoppers who stumbled upon Mercy House Global and our cute fair trade product, most of you are readers. And many of you are donors and make everything we do to empower women in Kenya and around the world possible.

When my husband and I returned from our first Sabbatical last week, we felt rested and ready for another decade of serving. But I don't think we were prepared for the attack the enemy had waiting on us. We returned home to some overwhelming challenges—we lost a couple hundred Fair Trade Friday club members this summer; we stepped out into faith to create wholesale lines (and many dignified jobs) and our expectations have not been met; we need thousands of dollars in monthly commitments from donors to meet our monthly budget; we had to allocate $25,000, money normally reserved for operations, to repair one of our maternity homes in Kenya due to flooding; too much product in inventory as we endeavored to continue providing jobs; the list goes on.

We have stood on holy ground for 9 years now. We have watched God do the impossible again and again. And today, we need Him to do it one more time. We need a miracle. First, we humbly ask for your prayers. We know that Mercy House belongs to God. We have never proclaimed to even know what we are doing, but we are doing our best.[6]

I was thinking about this book a lot while we rested in the mountains. Our souls were renewed, the empty places were filled. I cleared my head, postponed my to-do list, and I met Jesus there.

And honestly, I was stunned and wildly disappointed to return home ready to pick up where I left off only to discover an enormous mountain.

But mostly, I was disappointed in me. Because, of course, there's an impossible, unscalable, discouraging mountain looming in front of me. Why did I forget that God meets me in the mountains, on the difficult climbs, at the place when I'm most desperate for him? That he proves himself and is glorified by miraculously moving the mountains in our way?

"Truly I tell you, if anyone says to this mountain, 'Go, throw yourself into the sea,' and does not doubt in their heart but believes that what they say will happen, it will be done for them" (Mark 11:23). I am thanking him for the valley reprieve, and I'm ready to climb. I'm willing to bet there's a mountain or two in your way. Don't quit. Keep believing. You were meant to move mountains.

Something changed in me that day. I didn't quit, but I did give up. I stopped striving. I quit trying to keep Mercy House going. I decided that I couldn't sustain it a moment longer. God often keeps the circumstances the same. He doesn't move the mountains—he moves us. I decided when I wrote those words that I would persevere in trusting him, even if it meant that he didn't move the mountain in our way. I was willing to close the doors to Mercy House Global for good. I had been obedient, and that was all he asked of us.

God answered our prayers. He moved mountains of product and moved donors to give, and we will keep going until he says to stop.

But why do we have to struggle? Romans 5:1–5 says:

> Therefore, since we have been justified through faith, we have peace with God through our Lord Jesus Christ, through whom we have gained access by faith into this grace in which we now stand. And we boast in the hope of the glory of God. Not only so, but we also glory in our sufferings, because we know that suffering produces perseverance; perseverance, character; and character, hope. And hope does not put us to shame, because God's love has been poured out into our hearts through the Holy Spirit, who has been given to us.

I learned some important lessons during this season. One of the most important was centered on striving. As I've said before, I tend to be a workaholic. Even before writing books or starting Mercy House Global, I always had a side job, hustled home businesses, and created work for myself. I enjoy work. But the downside is I'm constantly thinking, planning, and striving. During our first sabbatical, I vowed it wouldn't be the last. I saw how long it took me to turn off the thoughts consuming me. I started being more intentional about practicing Sabbath. It's not always on a Sunday, and it's not usually spiritual, but practicing rest is now a priority. I am challenged and convicted by these words: "If you don't take a Sabbath, something is wrong. You're doing too much, you're being too much in charge. You've got to quit, one day a week, and just watch what God is doing when you're not doing anything."[7]

Hope

During Madison's Thanksgiving break her freshman year of college, I recalled our challenging summer and how no one had told me that sending my firstborn off to college would change things. It changed the number of people at our dinner table and the sibling dynamic. Even decorating our Christmas tree felt different because we had only a small window to do it in together. Our little family unit would never be the same again. It's not worse in any way—it may be better—but believe me, it's different. In a way, this letting go has taught me a lot about longing and hope. For the first time, I understood what Psalm 127:3–4 means: "Children are indeed a heritage from the LORD, and the fruit of the womb is His reward. Like arrows in the hand of a warrior, so are children born in one's youth" (BSB). I sent my arrow out, and for a time it seemed like there was one less in my quiver, but every time she returned home, I got to hear incredible stories of how she was making her mark on the world. Instead of her leaving filling me with dread, this truth filled me with hope.

Nor did anyone tell me that transitioning my beautiful child out of our home would change the way I parent the kids still at home. It's made me a better mom—more patient, more reflective, less uptight, less controlling. It's helped me to relax and relish my children more because I know what's coming. No one told me that I would live in this bitter-sweet intersection of watching my child thrive outside of my care and longing to have her back home at the same time—knowing that neither of us would be content if I got my way. No one told me that it would be fun and hilarious watching her learn and experience new things away from home. (This week she asked me how long it would take to microwave a turkey. I didn't hesitate to answer her prank question—two hours, rotate every fifteen minutes—because I totally believed this was a cooking lesson she needed to experience.)

No one told me how much easier it would be for my newly budget-conscious, work-study college kid to spend my money than hers. (If I'm within a one-hundred mile radius, she wants me to put gas in her car.) No one told me that the happier they are the less you hear from them (or that I would become a social-media stalker, hanging on bits and pieces of her active life).

No one told me that my young adult would be making huge decisions every day or how hard it would be for her to come back home and be my child. No one told me how much I would cherish and live for the moments when all my babies are together in the same car or in the same room under the same roof. No one told me that I would move heaven and earth to make those moments happen. No one told me that this parenting thing is beautiful and brutal on a mom's heart. No one told me that this season of stretching and surviving and soaring would bring me back to hope.

MOUNTAINTOP MOMENT

So, then, what is the purpose of our trials? We know we will face obstacles and challenges in life. We understand the enemy is relentless, and he will remind us of our failures and speak lies and discouragement into our hearts. We wonder where God is in the storm and often experience hurt and anger, but it's okay because we are reminded that God is with us. He is in control when things feel out of control. He wants us to trust him. God comforts us in our hard and heartbreaking seasons, and he brings good from the bad in our lives. He is refining us. It may not happen in the way we want it to, but God will move the mountains in our lives.

1. Read James 1.
2. Reflect on Martha Washington's positive approach to life's problems: "I am still determined to be cheerful and to be happy, in whatever situation I may be; for I have also learnt, from experience, that the greater part of our happiness or misery depends upon our dispositions, and not upon our circumstances."[8] How can you change your disposition in the face of the impossible?
3. How can you allow an inner action to happen in the middle of your trials so that even if your circumstances don't change, you do?

Journal

4

Jesus Changes Everything

Worship of Jesus is rather harmless and risk-free;
actually following Jesus changes everything.

Richard Rohr

When Terrell and I were gifted a trip to Israel to tour the
Holy Land, we were overwhelmed with gratitude. It had
been a dream of ours for decades, but it didn't seem possible in this expensive season of life with one in college, another about to graduate high school, and the youngest being
homeschooled—all on nonprofit salaries. The trip came a couple of months after our sabbatical and on the heels of a dark
and troubling season for our family. We had been mountain
climbing for months, and we were weary. I knew that the Bible
referred to mountains often, but after a quick Google search,
I was surprised to learn mountains are mentioned more than
five hundred times in the Bible. Author Joe Paprocki wrote
in an article on Busted Halo that "mountains have a logical

religious symbolism for Jewish and Christian cultures since they are 'closer to God' who dwells in the heavens. . . . As a result, God often reveals himself on a mountaintop in the text."[1]

As I prepared for the trip, which after eight days in Israel would conclude with a visit to Kenya, I desperately needed God to reveal himself to me again. I didn't realize the extravagance of the gift until I was sitting on a giant bed on my layover in Germany between my trips to Israel and Kenya when I tried to find the words to describe what it meant to walk where Jesus stepped.

If you've been there, you know what I mean when I say it feels impossible to describe. How do you explain sleeping next to the Sea of Galilee near Nazareth where Jesus grew up, riding in a boat on the same water he calmed, the same water on which he walked and overfilled fishing nets? How can I describe touching Herod's palace walls and dipping my toes in springs in the dessert where King Saul pursued David and in the Jordan River where John the Baptist baptized Jesus? How do I explain what it felt like to stand where King David, Jonathan, and Gideon stood?

I looked over the city Jesus wept for and walked the Palm Sunday and the Via Dolorosa roads that signified the beginning and end of his public ministry. I sat on the temple steps where Jesus taught and walked the Temple Mount where he angered the religious leaders. I stood at the walls that divide the Old City and tucked prayers where those around me wailed. I touched the stone walls where my Savior spent his first night in Bethlehem and the cold rock dungeon walls where he spent the last night of his life in Jerusalem. I wept where he was whipped, prayed where he was crucified, and rejoiced at the empty tomb.

In my journal, I wrote:

After stopping at the Jordan River this morning, we traveled through Samaria and Judea to the desert where Masada (which means "fortress"), King Herod's fortress, was carved on the side of the mountain before Christ was born. It's directly across from the Dead Sea.

In the dry, blistering heat, we learned that Herod's paranoia and fear pushed him to fortify himself and so many others behind the walls where the Romans would eventually reach them. The Jews were outnumbered and surrounded, but instead of being captured and becoming slaves, they killed themselves. It was a sad place, with oppressive heat, and it offered an eerie parallel to how Jews in Israel also have the odds stacked against them, pressed on every side by their enemies.

We traveled just a few miles down the road to En Gedi, and I nearly missed an incredible lesson (another hour hike in the desert sounded hot and exhausting). But as my pastor read from 1 Samuel 24, I learned that En Gedi is the place where King Saul pursued David and David had mercy and spared his life when he could have easily killed his enemy.

In the middle of this dry, desolate region, there is incredible lush landscape with multiple waterfalls and streams in the desert. It's a literal oasis. It made all the Scriptures about blooming in the dry places come alive (hello, soul).

As I climbed and dipped my toes in the cold, refreshing water, I thought about Herod's physical fortress and how it ultimately didn't protect them. And then there is David who said—maybe in this place I stood—"The LORD is my rock, and my fortress, and my deliverer; my God, my strength, in whom I will trust; my buckler, and the horn of my salvation, and my high tower" (Ps. 18:2 KJV).

When you tour Israel, you quickly learn that the Holy Land isn't the same as it was in Jesus's days. Cities are built on top of cities, and every year there are major archaeological discoveries in Jerusalem. Much of where Jesus walked is now underground because of civilizations raising the topography of the city, and historians and theologians debate the accuracy of sites. But in most cases, the mountains are for sure. Although the terrain has changed, the mountains remain. I walked on Mount Moriah, now called the Temple Mount, where Abraham offered Isaac (Gen. 22). I saw Mount Gilboa where Saul and his sons were killed (1 Sam. 31). I stood on Mount Carmel where Elijah called down fire from heaven (1 Kings 18:20–38). I sat on a rock on the mountain where Jesus taught the Beatitudes (Matt. 5:1–12), and I stood on the Mount of Olives, which overlooks Jerusalem, where Jesus ascended into heaven (Acts 1:9–12). I can no longer read passages such as Psalm 125:2 the same: "As the mountains surround Jerusalem, so the LORD surrounds his people, from this time forth and forevermore" (ESV).

I learned about geography and generations of God's chosen people. I learned about the letter of the law and walked the labyrinth of tunnels under Jerusalem. I learned about holy hills and the horrible holocaust that destroyed six million Jews. I learned a thousand things I didn't know, and what I did know came alive in a new way. I learned about the mountains of the Bible and the people who moved them.

But mostly, I learned the incredible truth that I hope you will learn too: *Jesus changed everything.* He altered history and heads of government. He changed geography and generations. He didn't just change the laws; he fulfilled them.

He didn't come to make bad people good; he came to make dead people alive. He exposed and revealed people's hearts; he pushed and prodded with parables; he shocked and surprised by doing the miraculous.

When Jesus came to earth the first time, he changed everything, and the incredible news is that, all these thousands of years later, he's now changing us. I was reminded at every historical spot and spiritual place that Jesus was killed because he was changing everything, and it terrified the people of his time. Everything stays the same without him, but nothing is the same with Jesus.

Jesus Changes How We Worship

One of the most powerful lessons I learned while in Israel was at an unexpected stop. It was raining hard, and so we postponed our outdoor tourist stop and escaped the rain in an ancient synagogue close to fifteen hundred years old. As we stood on a viewing ledge around the room to see the detail of the mosaic floor, it was easy to spot the tiny tiles that formed a massive zodiac in the center of the room. As the historian explained, this was a blasphemous and uncommon image in a holy temple, but it was a popular symbol in the culture at the time that Jewish people experienced freedom of worship. It was a startling and profound reminder of what humans do when we are not being oppressed—we let culture dictate who we become. How ironic it is to compare ancient history to modern society. The church today is easily influenced by modern trends and newly conceived truths, and we often follow what culture demands, even at the expense of the absolute truth we find in the Bible.

In *Letters to the Church*, Francis Chan wrote about how watered down the church has become because of the lack of persecution.

> I recall when my daughter and I went to an underground gathering in China years ago. Young people were praying so passionately, begging God to send them to the most dangerous places. They were actually hoping to die as martyrs! I had never seen anything like it. I still can't get over the fearless passion for Jesus that this church embodied.
>
> As they shared stories of persecution, I sat in amazement and asked for more stories. After a while, they asked why I was so intrigued. I told them that the church in America was nothing like this. I can't tell you how embarrassing it was to try to explain to them that people attend 90-minute services once a week in buildings, and that's what we call "church." I told them about how people switch churches if they find better teaching, or more exciting music, or more robust programs for their kids.
>
> As I described church life in America, they began to laugh. Not just small chuckles—they were laughing hysterically. I felt like a standup comedian, but I was literally just describing the American church as I've experienced it. They found it laughable that we could read the same Scriptures they were reading and then create something so incongruent.[2]

This story makes me sad and embarrassed for the church. Maybe it makes you feel the same way. Our first-world lives are often filled with ease and comfort while the lives of our neighbors around the globe are filled with desperation and difficulties. Our problems as first-world Christians are not the world's problems.

This past year, I returned from Kenya on a Saturday, the day between Good Friday and Easter. I found myself in between two worlds—the one in my culture where Easter is celebrated with three forty-five-minute church services, an Easter egg hunt, and long lines at popular restaurants, and the one in Sri Lanka where worshipers at three Christian churches were murdered by militant suicide bomber radicals while attending Easter services. While one isn't responsible for the other, it should remind us that the cost of following Jesus is higher for some.

I don't want to be persecuted any more than you do. But Francis Chan points to dozens of Scriptures that say persecution is part of the Christian's life.

> I have heard this all my life. "Now, the reason we are not getting persecuted is because we live in America." I don't believe that. If you are not being persecuted, it's because you purposely avoid persecution. If Jesus lived in America, He would be persecuted. You know why? Because He didn't know how to keep His mouth shut. He spoke up. Remember, the disciples had a chance to avoid persecution. The religious leaders told them, "Just stop preaching about Jesus." Peter replied, "You judge for yourself. Who am I going to obey, you or God?" . . . This suffering stuff is in every book of the New Testament. It's all over. . . . The message of Christianity is that you will suffer for Jesus—and He is worth it![3]

Jesus Changes How We Live

Every Christmas, I buy my kids new pajamas. It's our Christmas Eve tradition—go to church, come home and read the Christmas story, give kids embarrassing matching pajamas

and a new family board game, and sip hot chocolate in ri-
diculous plaid pants while usually arguing over who is really
winning the game.

When I clicked on the internet to snag the best deal, I remembered the commitment my nineteen-year-old daughter
and I had made two years before to buy only fair-trade or
secondhand clothes. Over the past year, our wardrobes have
slowly changed. It's been hard and really good. We have less,
we have more—I had a choice to make.

Would I buy what was easy, quick, and cheap, or would
I use my purchase power to literally set people free? Would
I shop in ignorance, or would I research before I bought?
Would I possibly contribute to modern-day slavery by buying something made in a sweatshop, or would I spend a little
more in an effort to provide freedom? This is why most of
my clothes come from thrift stores and secondhand shops.
I buy fewer new things because ethically made clothing isn't
cheap.

I thought about the irony of how many of my past Christmas morning celebrations kept people in bondage on the
birthday of the One who came to set us free. Yeah, I'm a
real shopping delight. But if I run a nonprofit built on empowering women and I don't shop with purpose, who will?
This isn't a challenge for you to accept my own personal
convictions, but I do hope it makes you think about what
you buy.

More times than I can count, I have sat in the homes of
women who sold their children into slavery because they
knew they would survive, even if it cost them their freedom. I have met women around the globe who are making
impossible, desperate choices. And while I know that my

Christmas pajama purchase isn't enough to solve the problem of modern slavery or fast fashion, tell that to the one person my purchase liberates.

So, my kids got ethical, matching pajama pants that Christmas. They cost more, but pajamas that set people free are a real thing; so is stunning handcrafted jewelry, woven rugs, and handmade paper cards. Every purchase we make for our homes and families can't be fair trade, but when they can be, shouldn't they be? There are so many items that do provide help and hope, and I have made it my life's work to tell you about them. When we know the truth, we are responsible. When we have the power to set people free with our purchases, we should.

What I'm really proposing here is that if Jesus truly changes how we live, he will also change how we spend. We will care about justice because he cares about justice. We will acknowledge that some of the forty million slaves in our world today who do not walk in freedom could be in bondage due to America's consumerism.

On the second-year anniversary of starting Mercy House, I got a tattoo on the arch of my foot. It hurt, and for weeks every step I took was a reminder of the painful course correction I was on. "What, oh man, do I require of you? Act justly, love mercy, and walk humbly" is burned onto the flesh of my foot because God etched Micah 6:8 onto the flesh of my heart. I care about justice because God asks me to.

I know these aren't easy words to swallow. I get how hard it is, and I understand it costs us more. I know I'm talking about flipping things upside down—or is it really flipping them rightside up? But if Christians—who value justice and stand for righteousness—aren't buying fair trade, if believers aren't supporting fair purchases, are we really living fair lives? Has encountering Jesus really changed how we live?

> All our homes tell a story. Our homes are always either telling fair trade stories or unfair stories.
>
> Every blanket, every mat, every spoon, every plate—in every one of our homes—began somewhere in the world. . . .
>
> What if your home could tell a story of grace?
>
> Grace given, grace received, grace passed forward and given again.
>
> The welcome mats under our feet, the steaming mugs in our hands, the full bowls on our tables, could tell a grace story—a story of fair trade, a story of life change, a story of saving, Gospel grace. Stories that empower a sister, change the lives of a whole family, free another soul from darkness, offer the sheltering roof of amazing grace.[4]

We can't change what has been done. We waste our time regretting what has already been bought and spent. But every new day is an opportunity to let the greatness of the gospel—who Jesus is—change how we shop and what we do. When we encounter Jesus, he changes how we live. If knowing and serving him doesn't change how we live, do we really know him?

Jesus Changes Who We Are

I picked up three small smooth stones from the shore of the Sea of Galilee for my kids and tucked them into my pocket. Terrell and I got in a fishing boat that looked like a replica from Jesus's day. The water was still like glass and surrounded by mountains. I thought about the mountains

I've climbed and those that still loom ahead, large and insurmountable. I thought about the storm that tends to rage inside as I looked out on the water Jesus walked on and calmed. I reminded myself he was in the boat with us. I love the story we find in Mark 4:

> That day when evening came, he said to his disciples, "Let us go over to the other side." Leaving the crowd behind, they took him along, just as he was, in the boat. There were also other boats with him. A furious squall came up, and the waves broke over the boat, so that it was nearly swamped. Jesus was in the stern, sleeping on a cushion. The disciples woke him and said to him, "Teacher, don't you care if we drown?"
>
> He got up, rebuked the wind and said to the waves, "Quiet! Be still!" Then the wind died down and it was completely calm.
>
> He said to his disciples, "Why are you so afraid? Do you still have no faith?"
>
> They were terrified and asked each other, "Who is this? Even the wind and the waves obey him!" (vv. 35–41)

Pastor Todd Phillips teaches in his Bible study *Keep Climbing* that Jesus invited the fishermen turned disciples to the place where they were most comfortable: the water. A huge storm met the boat in the water and the disciples panicked in total fear. They cried out to Jesus, but he was asleep in the middle of the storm. "Every one of us goes through silence in our lives. With God, he's silent for a reason. He wants to test the authenticity of our faith."[5] Silence is a hard part of the journey. Jesus was in the boat, but he was silent. Having Jesus in the boat was enough, but they didn't have enough faith.

Jesus calmed the storm. Sometimes he provides immediate, tangible miracles. Other times he is silent to test our faith. Is our faith dependent on what he does for us or on who he is?

How many times have I been afraid, scared out of my mind, in a total panic, and my faith minuscule, and I'm oblivious to Jesus right next to me? Jesus miraculously calmed the storm. But he doesn't work the same way every time. Pastor Phillips believes God moves our mountains in three distinct ways:[6]

1. *Intervention*: We see Jesus intervene on behalf of the scared disciples in the boat and immediately calm the waters and resolve the situation. They asked and he moved the mountain. Throughout the Bible, we see examples of God's immediate, miraculous movement. It's jaw-dropping, incredible, and often unbelievable. We cling to the stories of God splitting the Red Sea, of walls falling down, and of Jesus multiplying the fish and loaves. We long to see him perform miracles in our lives—raise the dead to life, heal terminal cancer, reconcile families. We want Jesus to intervene for us. We read about God intervening on Paul and Silas's behalf in Acts 16 when they were imprisoned and praising God. "Suddenly there was such a violent earthquake that the foundations of the prison were shaken. At once all the prison doors flew open, and everyone's chains came loose" (v. 27). No one escaped; instead, Paul and Silas prayed with the jailer to be saved. We are encouraged at God's miraculous intervention. But as we know, he doesn't always work this way.

2. *Inner action*: God moves mountains not by changing our circumstances but by changing us instead. Pastor Phillips gives the example of Paul, once again in prison, but this time there is no earthquake or chains dropping off. Paul spent several years as a prisoner in Rome, but he didn't let his imprisonment defeat him. He appears in his writings to be joyful in spite of his circumstances, and scholars believe he wrote seven letters of the New Testament during this time. He took advantage of the time he was in prison and allowed God to speak through him. God often leaves our circumstances unchanged. He doesn't move the mountain—he moves us. He asks us to go *through* in order to overcome.

3. *Interaction*: Both God and man act: "Interaction is where God empowers us to do something in the situation. . . . He helps us help ourselves," writes Pastor Phillips.[7] I love this definition of interaction. It's the faith-in-action formula that requires our obedience and trust that he will be there with us as we take a step of faith to follow him.

MOUNTAINTOP MOMENT

In 2018, I traveled with a team from Mercy House to introduce art to our teen moms in Kenya. The Swahili word *sanaa* means "art." My daughter Madison was one of the art teachers who taught these beautiful and eager artists how to hold paintbrushes, sketch self-portraits, draw intricate shapes, and dream again. I lack the words to describe how God is using art to heal and provide hope where both are needed. I held back tears as I watched my daughter teach her peers how to watercolor gorgeous mountain landscapes. One of those paintings became the cover of this book. Little did I know that as she showed them how to paint the depth and realism of mountains, our family would step into its shadows again. The last few years have taught me the beauty of these words from Richard Dahlstrom, pastor of Bethany Community Church: "Thankfully, God has shown us that hope, in its million different forms, always springs from three primary colors: justice, mercy, and love."[8]

What is it about mountains and the spiritual life? Yes, we see proof they were a part of the landscape of the Bible. But the link between mountains and worship that we find in God's Word should make us pause, reflect, and ask, How has Jesus—who changed everything—changed me?

> God is our refuge and strength,
> a very present help in trouble.
> Therefore we will not fear, though the earth should change,
> though the mountains shake in the heart of the sea;
> though its waters roar and foam,
> though the mountains tremble with its tumult.

There is a river whose streams make glad the city of
    God,
      the holy habitation of the Most High.
God is in the midst of the city; it shall not be moved;
      God will help it when the morning dawns.
The nations are in an uproar, the kingdoms totter;
      he utters his voice, the earth melts.
The LORD of hosts is with us;
      the God of Jacob is our refuge.

Come, behold the works of the LORD;
      see what desolations he has brought on the earth.
He makes wars cease to the end of the earth;
      he breaks the bow, and shatters the spear;
      he burns the shields with fire.
"Be still, and know that I am God!
      I am exalted among the nations,
      I am exalted in the earth."
The LORD of hosts is with us;
      the God of Jacob is our refuge. (Ps. 46 NRSV)

1. Reflect on Psalm 46.
2. Is your life different because you know Jesus? Has he changed everything?
3. Write down a couple of practical first steps you can take in your daily life to live against the grain of culture.

Journal

5

Oh, We of Little Faith

Faith is not believing in my own unshakeable belief. Faith is believing an unshakeable God when
everything in me trembles and quakes.

Beth Moore

Mom, one of my eyes is blurry." I looked up from cooking breakfast to see one of my kids squinting one eye
and then the other. The words surprised me.

"What do you mean?" I asked. I had stopped stirring the
eggs. We were in the middle of that sabbatical I told you
about. We were more than seven hundred miles from home
and still had two weeks left.

"I don't know. It's weird. I just woke up and one eye is
blurry." I called the doctor and they asked a few questions.
They said blurry vision was possible with dry eyes in the
dry climate we were staying in and recommended using re-
wetting drops.

I made a mental note to make an appointment with an eye doctor for all my kids when we got back home. They told me wearing glasses was in, and they all hoped for a pair.

Once back home, we shifted into college prep mode. If you have ever sent a kid away to college, you know how long the prep list is. My child hadn't mentioned blurry vision again, and in all the hustle, I'd forgotten to make that family eye appointment. Our days were filled with shopping for items needed for a dorm room, cleaning out closets, and sorting mounds of papers and projects dating back to junior high. We steadily worked our way down the massive "I'm moving into a dorm" list. We weren't just getting Madison's things ready for a new home; we were also getting her bedroom ready for a new person.

About six months earlier, a pastor friend from a foreign country had asked us to help find his daughter, Yana, who was the same age as Madison, a place to live. Yana had gotten a student visa to study in America and needed a family to host her. Although we had never met her, we loved and respected the gospel work her parents were doing. A picture of their family had hung in our kitchen for nearly a decade as a reminder to pray for them. When our friend brought up the prayer request, Terrell and I knew we would have an empty bedroom in our house. We explained the situation to our kids and showed them the old photo, pointing out tiny Yana. Before we could even finish, Madison said, "She should take my room! This is the right thing to do." We agreed and hugged Madison. It did feel like the next right step for our family. This is how we lived—open and ready to walk through doors that opened in front of us. We talked about the benefits and challenges we might face, but God had been showing me that the heart of generosity is to share what we have. We would have an empty bed, and Yana needed one to sleep in.

So Madison's college prep list also became Yana's welcome home list with only a week separating the one leaving home and the one moving in. Move-in day was less than a week away, when again blurry vision was casually mentioned over dinner. I mentally kicked myself for forgetting to make an appointment as I scrambled to squeeze one more thing onto the list.

For the past year, I'd been planning a return trip to the wholesale market in New York City to launch new Mercy House products in our wholesale line. But when I got the dates for the market, I discovered they were the exact dates I would be moving Madison into her dorm room. For hours, I looked at flights and tried to juggle doing both. I told myself and my daughter I could get her packed up and ready to go the week before I left for NYC and then hurry home afterward and drive her that night to her college campus two and a half hours away. My daughter said she understood because she knows how amazing the market is and how important the event is to me.

But important events are never more important than people. After a couple of days of trying to convince myself I could do it all, my gut wouldn't stop reminding me of these words attributed to Mother Teresa: "You see this is where love begins—at home in the family."[1] Sometimes you get to preach truth, and other times you get to swallow it. And sometimes when you really want to change the world, you just need to go home and love your family.

When my daughter got home late from work one night that week, she came to my bedroom and sprawled across my bed.

She was wiped out from six hours on her feet at her retail shift. I told her I wouldn't be heading to NYC for the wholesale market after all. She shot up. "Why, Mom? You have to go!"

Oh my heart. I looked at my little world changer who had made more sacrifices than most teenagers her age, and I felt so much compassion for her for giving me up to Mercy House one more time.

"I'd rather be with you. I think we're going to need the week to say goodbye and get you ready for your new adventure," I replied. The look on her face made me feel like I was truly changing the world. When we love our families well and really listen to their needs and respond the best way we know how, that's exactly what we are doing.

I thought of all this as I sat with my kids for the unplanned eye appointment, and I shook my head, wondering how I would have juggled a trip across the United States and an unexpected doctor appointment all in the same week I was moving my firstborn into her dorm. God knew that I would need to be home with my family. I reminded myself that his timing is perfect, even in the middle of questioning it.

My kids were called back for their vision tests, one at a time. About fifteen minutes later, the doctor called me back with a very concerned look on his face. "Mrs. Welch, something is seriously wrong with your child's left eye. There has been significant loss of vision, and it's not correctible with glasses. I have called a retinal specialist. It is urgent." He tossed out a lot of big words, but the only one I would remember from the appointment was *blindness*.

The cold shock of the moment will stay with me forever. I was terrified. Are parents ever prepared for words like these from a doctor? Immediately, worry set in, and I could see the concern on my children's faces too. I didn't know what to say. It's hard to reassure your children everything will be okay when you wonder if your words are a complete lie. But I gave a shaky smile and squeezed shoulders and did exactly that because that's what moms do. We try to hold everything together even when we are falling apart on the inside.

The next seventy-two hours were a total whirlwind. We spent a full day with a specialist. They ran test after test, probing and searching for a reason for the sudden eye condition. They asked a hundred questions about family history, eye injuries, blunt force, and pain. I texted a couple of family members and friends and asked them to pray. My hand shook as I hunted for each letter. "Please pray. I'm scared."

One of my sweet friends who has been a prayer warrior for my family texted back one word that made the tears flow: "Mountains." I fought back the tears when they called our name, and we followed the nurse into a room.

The doctor showed us on the monitor what a healthy eye would look like. It dipped like a valley. And then he pulled up the image of my child's left eye, and I bit my lip and let out an audible gasp. Instead of a valley, the area behind the retina looked like a mountain. The doctor said, "This is a mountain of swelling, and if you had not come in, your child would be blind in this eye in a matter of weeks."

We would soon be moving my daughter into her college dorm, and I was struggling to even stand up straight. I wrote the following on my blog on August 16, 2018—move-in day:

I woke up at 5 A.M. in a hotel room on my daughter's last day at "home." It was college dorm move-in day and our cars were packed and she was ready to fly.

It was still dark in the room but light enough to see that my son was hanging off the air mattress on the floor and our daughters were still asleep in the bed next to my husband and me. I quietly slipped out of bed and stood over them and tried to memorize the moment.

That's when I noticed my girls were holding hands, asleep.

For weeks, we have all been feeling the epic shift that was happening in our home. Preparing your child to leave is the true definition of the word bittersweet. I just can't think of another word to describe the excitement and the sorrow all tangled up together.

This letting go is a slow grieving process filled with joy and fear. It's a paradox of conflicting emotions. It's hard and oh, so good.

We were out of the hotel by 7:30 in the morning for our daughter's 7:45 slotted move-in time. As we rounded the corner in front of her dorm, we could hear the chanting and cheering and I could feel the lump swell in my throat.

We rolled down the windows and we could hear the crowd around our car saying these two words over and over, "Welcome, home. Welcome, home." I squeezed her hand, her car door opened, and the welcome team ushered her out of the car to get her room key. In a matter of seconds, the upperclassmen had carried off her boxes to her room and she was gone and I was alone in the car, husband and kids following behind.

These words were echoing in my ears and heart. Welcome home.

All the planning and prepping, the arguments and cherished moments brought us to this moment when I realized yes, this was her new home, and that's when I lost it.

I could barely drive to park the car for the tears. It would be the only five minutes I would be alone until we were back home later that night. I sobbed.

I hid my red eyes behind my sunglasses and our family spent the next three hours making our daughter's room adorable (she basically just told all of us what to do).

It was perfect. And hard, and oh, so good. More than a half dozen times, I swallowed the lump in my throat and stopped the flow of tears that were threatening as we put her parking sticker on her car and visited her mailbox and did all the things to seal the deal on this big transition.

We knew goodbye (which we had already dubbed "see you later") was coming and none of us wanted to say it. The five of us stood in her dorm, held hands in a circle and prayed the sweetest words over our beautiful, strong and incredible girl.

It was perfect. And hard, and oh so good. Right before we drove the three hours home, I whispered in her ear, "Welcome home, honey."[2]

Reality was waiting for us back at home. I can't say how every parent feels when one of their children receives an unexpected, life-changing diagnosis. I can only tell you that for me, it was a shocking, gut-wrenching blow to my world. It stopped me in my tracks and deeply changed me in ways I can't explain. This was a mountain we didn't know how to climb, and we certainly didn't want to scale it. If you had asked me a week before if I believed God could do anything, I would have confidently said yes. I have seen him do the impossible over and over again. But that first night at home, with a new, scary diagnosis on our lips and my baby curled beside me, I was terrified of the unknown, and I clung to every promise I could remember.

I told Terrell I wanted to anoint our child with oil and pray for healing. He agreed and started toward us. "No, I mean the kind of prayer that's in James 5." He nodded and went to the kitchen. I called everyone to our bedroom, and Terrell returned with an enormous bottle of olive oil. This really concerned our kids, and they had a lot of questions: "What are we going to do with that oil? Are you pouring it on our heads? Are we in a cult?" I tried not to laugh. It was a serious moment for our family, but I was so thankful for their humor.

I reassured them and pulled out my Bible and read James 5:14–16: "Is anyone among you sick? Let them call the elders of the church to pray over them and anoint them with oil in the name of the Lord. And the prayer offered in faith will make the sick person well; the Lord will raise them up. If they have sinned, they will be forgiven. Therefore confess your sins to each other and pray for each other so that you may be healed. The prayer of a righteous person is powerful and effective."

Terrell touched the oil to the forehead of our child, and we each took turns praying out loud for healing. I cried at the broken beauty of the moment and for as long as I live, I will never forget the moment our family trusted God to move this impossible mountain.

It was a brutal month—filled with doctor visits, tests, results, and fear. I don't think I've ever been more afraid. For the first few days, Terrell and I walked around in total shock. Nothing else mattered. I've heard from other parents that this is a new kind of normal. You become laser-focused on defeating the disease that is attacking your child.

We were just a month home from our sabbatical and weeks from the cash-flow crisis at Mercy House, and I found myself knocking on the door of a very dark place. Earlier in the summer while we were hiking in the mountains, my family wanted to keep climbing. I wanted to hide in the cleft of the rock. It was quiet and beautiful, and I took a deep breath, stretched out my legs, and rested while they kept going. That's when I saw the small opening in the rocks behind me. I bent down and peeked into the black hole and was surprised to see bright green plants growing in the darkness. I have thought about those little plants and their bad odds a hundred times since. It reminded me of words I had once read from author Sandra Kring: "The tiny seed knew that in order to grow, it needed to be dropped in the dirt, covered in darkness, struggle to reach the light."[3]

The timing of the news made it even more difficult. I wavered between worrying about my child, desperately missing my college kid, and putting on a brave face for our new houseguest and the rest of the family. But something utterly unexpected occurred in the middle of the darkness; we grew. Every curve ball thrown our way pushed us closer to Jesus. These words became a lifeline: "When . . . you are in tough times, you may feel like you've been buried, but the fact is, you've simply been planted. That means you're coming back."[4]

Literally in the middle of all of the uncertainty, Yana moved into our home. Behind closed doors, I struggled once again with the unlikely timing. I didn't have the strength or even desire to welcome her into our home. I was exhausted and afraid. I was consumed with simply putting one foot in front of another in the darkness. The atmosphere was heavy in our house, and who wants to move into that? But I clung to the sovereignty of God and trusted that he would redeem everything. A few weeks into her transition, I marveled at my hesitancy. The best way to describe Yana is to liken her to a rainbow. She entered our home during a dark season, but her contagious joy, easy nature, and darling personality were good for our family. God's timing is perfect—it isn't always easy and not always what we would choose, but he gives us what we need just when we need it.

In every other way, it was a brutal year—from challenging relationships to unexpected financial hardships to medical issues. I have been angry and afraid. I have felt hurt and hopeless. I have been uncomfortable and uncertain. My faith has been shaken, but I still believe God is faithful. In his book *Moving Mountains*, John Eldridge writes, "When we are in the darkness, we begin to feel like we have always been there. But it is not true. David reminds himself that God has been faithful in the past; God will be faithful again. He urges himself to put his hope in God because the morning will come."[5]

I have to tell you that I don't know the ending to this story. I don't know if I'll ever have mended relationships that don't cause me pain. I do know Terrell and I will face financial challenges again because our jobs at Mercy House require us to raise a huge amount of money every year. I don't know if my child will be healed, and I don't know what other hardships we may face. I don't know what other mountains may stand in my way. I just know that some days feel really dark.

MOUNTAINTOP MOMENT

Maybe you too are surrounded by uncertainty and overwhelmed by hardships, maybe even overcome by fear or darkness.

Think about Joel Osteen's words. Could it be that this darkness, this hard place, is the perfect place to grow?

> For God, who said, "Let light shine out of darkness," made his light shine in our hearts to give us the light of the knowledge of God's glory displayed in the face of Christ.
>
> But we have this treasure in jars of clay to show that this all-surpassing power is from God and not from us. We are hard pressed on every side, but not crushed; perplexed, but not in despair; persecuted, but not abandoned; struck down, but not destroyed. We always carry around in our body the death of Jesus, so that the life of Jesus may also be revealed in our body. For we who are alive are always being given over to death for Jesus' sake, so that his life may also be revealed in our mortal body. (2 Cor. 4:6–11)

1. Think about the passage from 2 Corinthians. Write down some ways that Christ shines in the darkness.
2. How can you look past your circumstances and ahead to where Jesus is leading you?
3. What are some ways you are growing in the desert place?

Journal

6

Permission to Grieve

Suffering is actually at the heart of the Christian story.

Tim Keller

I was in a heavy fog. I cried easily; I researched constantly; I carried the weight of the unknown around my neck like a heavy stone. This wasn't the first time I needed to grieve in my life, but it might have been the first time I needed permission to. I identified with the words of pastor and theologian Tim Keller in *Walking with God through Pain and Suffering*: "No matter what precautions we take, no matter how well we have put together a good life, no matter how hard we have worked to be healthy, wealthy, comfortable with friends and family, and successful with our career—something will inevitably ruin it."[1]

I have known heartache before—when my marriage nearly ended at the ten-year mark, when our youngest, Emerson, was born too early and fought for her life in intensive care for weeks, when we faced death and disaster in the early years of Mercy House. I have known hardships. But when I opened my heart to the suffering of the world through our work to empower marginalized women around the globe, I gained perspective. Perspective doesn't remove our suffering, but it changes how we see it. If there is a downside to perspective, it might look a lot like guilt. When you have witnessed the kind of suffering brought on by extreme poverty, trafficking, and child rape, it makes your problems seem much smaller.

I needed permission to grieve because sometimes emptying yourself of all that is pent up is the best way to climb a mountain. I was sharing what our family was going through with one of the few close friends I leaned on during this season. I didn't realize it, but I was qualifying the situation when I said, "I know it's not as bad as . . . ," and my friend called me on it. "Stop doing that, Kristen. It's okay to stop and feel the pain of this. It's shocking and unexpected, and you need to admit it. If you need permission to acknowledge this as suffering, here it is. It's okay for you to grieve."

Her words made me realize that minimizing my pain wasn't helping me overcome it. It was just prolonging it. I was talking one night on the phone with a friend who leads a global nonprofit and who knows something about suffering. Her family was suddenly and harshly expelled from their home and work overseas where they served and lived. She said well-meaning people offered ways to help them get over her pain, but no one really gave her permission to grieve.

Over several months, I slowly began to give myself permission to go to the grieving place inside of me and feel loss. I wrote things privately to Jesus. I cried until I couldn't cry anymore. While it didn't really accomplish anything at first, I at least started the process of emptying myself of expectations and pain. I shook my fist. I felt angry, and I loosened my death grip on control. And then something kind of beautiful and unexpected happened in my grief. I experienced a deeper compassion for those who suffer. Dealing with my pain helped me to see the pain of others more clearly. Embracing my sorrow showed me that Jesus was grieving with me. Every single thing we have faced and what we will endure in the future, our Lord experienced during his lifetime and on the cross. Second Corinthians 1:3–4 says, "Let us give thanks to the God and Father of our Lord Jesus Christ, the merciful Father, the God from whom all help comes! He helps us in all our troubles, so that we are able to help others who have all kinds of troubles, using the same help that we ourselves have received from God" (GNT).

Tim Keller's words in *Walking with God through Pain and Suffering* hit me between the eyes, and I began to see suffering in a completely new way.

> Jesus lost all his glory so that we could be clothed in it. He was shut out so we could get access. He was bound, nailed, so that we could be free. He was cast out so we could approach.
>
> And Jesus took away the only kind of suffering that can really destroy you: that is being cast away from God. He took that so that now all suffering that comes into your life will only make you great. A lump of coal under pressure becomes a diamond. And the suffering of a person in Christ only turns you into somebody gorgeous.[2]

I scribbled in the margins, "All the crap we are going through is making us beautiful." It wasn't my most eloquent moment, but it's still profound truth. The pressure from all sides that Paul writes about in 2 Corinthians 4:8–10 produces something: "We are hard pressed on every side, but not crushed; perplexed, but not in despair; persecuted, but not abandoned; struck down, but not destroyed. We always carry around in our body the death of Jesus, so that the life of Jesus may also be revealed in our body."

I love the lyrics from Hillsong: "You take our failure. You take our weakness. You set Your treasure in jars of clay. So take this heart, Lord."[3] We are fragile jars of clay. We break easily. Why do we work so hard to hold it together when falling apart is sometimes the next right thing? When we are crushed, we aren't ruined. We are revealing the diamond inside that all the external pressure has created. In her book *Unexpected*, Christine Caine writes, "Jesus always walks with us through our disappointment. Through our heartaches. Leading us to recover our wonder. Leading us to something better ahead."[4]

I am reminded of a couple of passages from Scripture. The first is 1 Peter 1:24–25: "All flesh is like grass and all its glory like the flower of grass. The grass withers, and the flower falls, but the word of the Lord remains forever" (ESV). The second is Matthew 6:25–30:

> Therefore I tell you, do not worry about your life, what you will eat or drink; or about your body, what you will wear. Is not life more than food, and the body more than clothes? Look at the birds of the air; they do not sow or reap or store away in barns, and yet your heavenly Father feeds them. Are you not much more valuable than they? Can any one of you by worrying add a single hour to your life? And why do you worry about clothes? See how the flowers of the field

grow. They do not labor or spin. Yet I tell you that not even Solomon in all his splendor was dressed like one of these. If that is how God clothes the grass of the field, which is here today and tomorrow is thrown into the fire, will he not much more clothe you—you of little faith?

Christine's words from her book *Undaunted* are so wise: "God deliberately chooses imperfect vessels—those who have been wounded, those with physical or emotional limitations. Then he prepares them to serve and sends them out *with their weakness still in evidence*, so that his strength can be made perfect in that weakness."[5] In her book *Unstoppable*, she explains:

> The Bible is full of ordinary people whom God called to his divine relay. Which of them, in their power, their resources, or their ways had what was required to do what God called them to do? Not one.
>
> Moses was told to lead his people from slavery, then was caught between Pharaoh's chariots and the Red Sea. Joshua was told to conquer the walled city of Jericho armed with nothing more than trumpets. Gideon was told to defeat the massive Midianite army after the Lord purposefully shrank his army from 32,000 men to only 300 armed with nothing more than trumpets, torches, and empty jars. Peter was beckoned by Jesus to get out of the boat and walk on water.
>
> Are you catching the theme here? Just like these people, when we learn to focus on who God is rather than on what we are not, we see that it is God who is working in us to do the very thing he has purposed to do in our lives. As we learn to run the race, accept his batons, and submit to his training, God's work in and through us is always growing

and increasing. Christ in us becomes an unstoppable force in our lives and is spilled out into the lives of others.[6]

I thought of something I read by my friend Ann Voskamp, author and Mercy House Global board member, on Facebook one day: "Your legs may be weary, your heart may be heavy, but whatever you are facing, it is always named Mt. Moriah—'the Lord will provide' (Gen. 22:14). Every mountain that you face, the Lord will level with sufficient grace."[7]

I was sitting in a coffee shop and flipped to Genesis 22 and reread the story of Abraham when God asked him to sacrifice his only son and then provided a miracle substitute. "So Abraham called that place The LORD Will Provide. And to this day it is said, 'On the mountain of the LORD it will be provided'" (v. 14).

In the middle of my grief and unanswered questions, I stood on Mount Moriah in Israel and couldn't help but think about the mountains we were facing. But I also marveled at where obedience will take us and how God always provides what we need. I don't know if you know this (I didn't), but current-day Mount Moriah doesn't even look like a mountain. It's flat and is located in the Old City of Jerusalem.

I learned this fact from *Voice in the Wilderness*: "When Jacob was fleeing from Esau, he had this vision of angels going up and down a ladder between Heaven and earth. God speaks to him . . . (Gen. 28:16–19). This is Mt. Moriah where Abraham met with God on the occasion of the sacrifice of Isaac (Gen. 22:2); where, also, Solomon built the temple (2 Chron. 3:1). Today, the so-called 'temple mount.'"[8]

In 2 Chronicles 3:1, we read that "Solomon began to build the temple of the LORD in Jerusalem on Mount Moriah." Today, many theologians believe it is the same location as the Temple Mount. It's the holiest spot in the world for Jews, Christians, and Muslims, and it's also the most sought after. It's why Orthodox Jews face the Wailing Wall—it's the closest they can get to this holy place, which is heavily guarded by armed Muslims who control the space behind the wall. It's also the spot at which many Christians believe the temple will one day be rebuilt. I think it's incredible that Mount Moriah—where Abraham obeyed and which means "The LORD Will Provide"—is the same place that many theologians believe the temple of God will be reestablished in the Holy City of God. It's amazing to even consider—but not at all surprising since God has always used weak, inadequate people to fulfill his great plan.

A friend who was attending the IF Gathering in February 2019, after hearing Christine Caine speak about something similar in the keynote address, commented that when Moses and the Israelites were pushed to the edge of the sea by their enemies, they faced the impossible. But Moses had a big stick and a bigger God. Sometimes God asks us to do crazy things for reasons we don't understand. He wants us to pick up the stick he's provided and trust him to part the waters.

I love Moses. I love his stutter, his insecurity, his low self-esteem. I love him because I can identify with a guy who wasn't a big deal, who wasn't qualified. Moses was ordinary and flawed, and yet he is a hero of our faith. He allowed God to use him, to be made perfect in his weakness.

I don't know what you're facing today, right now, this very moment as you read these words. I don't know what mountain is around the bend in your life. But I do know that life is full of ups and downs. I want you to know that you have permission to feel loss, sadness, disappointment, and grief in your situation. This is the first step in taking the right next step. We live in a fix-it culture that's consumed with a microwave, drive-thru mentality. But speeding up the process of grief doesn't help us get over our pain any sooner. Instead, it delays it. You will eventually grieve, and it might hit you when you least expect it. The opposite of grief isn't happiness. You have permission to be sad, to experience sorrow, if you need it. As Tim Keller says, "Secular culture says the meaning of life is to gain happiness. If that's true then suffering destroys meaning."[9] But God allows suffering in our lives so that we will know joy despite our circumstances.

It's okay to walk through a season of not being okay. I knew I wasn't alone. A dear friend and I tried to reschedule getting together for three months due to sickness, sadness, or both, and we were overdue for a good visit. But the more I tried, the more she hesitated, and I could tell she wasn't okay. I tried to reconnect with her: I suggested fun activities, reminded her of good times, sent her inspiring Scripture. When we finally met up, I knew she was having more than a bad day; she was having a sad season.

She didn't say much, and I got only an occasional head nod or shrug. As I sat there in silence, I thought back to days when I hadn't been okay. Some days I could name the pain I felt, and other days I could not. When I thought of my own pain, I remembered what I needed the most. So I did what I should have done in the first place: I hugged her and whispered in her ear, "It's okay to not be okay."

She sighed in relief. Permission to not be okay is sometimes exactly what we need. We sat in comfortable silence for a long time. I reminded her that God loved these days the best—the ones we can't fix on our own—because he is there with us. He doesn't always change our circumstances, and we don't always feel something new, but we aren't alone.

She wiped away a single tear and whispered, "Thank you." When I left, I felt I hadn't done much, but it was enough.

Today, you might not be okay. You might be looking at a scary diagnosis, experiencing a financial disaster, or struggling with a wayward child. You might be facing a mountain of sadness or impossibility. You might be walking through a valley of despair. You might not even know why you aren't okay.

At these moments, we do everything we can think of to resolve the struggle in our souls. And life sort of feels like quicksand—the harder we struggle, the deeper we sink. The days are dark and lonely, and our souls are crushed by the heaviness of despair. On these days, sometimes I see how easy my life appears in the eyes of those who live such difficult ones, and I push away my pain out of guilt. While I admit that I've made my life harder in an effort to ease the burden of their lives, I also confess that I get weary in well doing. There are many days I'm not okay.

But one thing can refresh and renew and save our souls, and that is the Word of God. Yet often it's the last place we turn. It seems crazy to think a book with words can be the answer, but God's Word is alive, and it cuts to the broken places and heals what we cannot. Our situation or struggle may not dissolve overnight, but we can find solace and comfort in the words he's given us.

The LORD is my shepherd, I shall not want.
    He makes me lie down in green pastures;
he leads me beside still waters;
    he restores my soul.
He leads me in right paths
    for his name's sake.

Even though I walk through the darkest valley,
    I fear no evil;
for you are with me;
    your rod and your staff—
    they comfort me. (Ps. 23:1–4 NRSV)

MOUNTAINTOP MOMENT

I don't know what your mountain looks like. You have permission to grieve what you are going through. It doesn't change your situation; it doesn't lighten your load. But it is the first step. I grieve for what my family has faced, and I grieve for what I can't fix. I grieve because it's the path to healing. I don't know what will come next, but I believe the Lord will provide what I need because that is what he does on the mountains.

1. Do you need permission to grieve? What does that look like for you? Is there someone you need to talk to or something you need to write down or allow yourself to feel?
2. What do you need God to provide? Is it resources or something less tangible like time or energy? Write it down.
3. What has God given you? Moses had a stutter. What do you have that makes your mountain climbing feel impossible? It's often easier to look at what we don't have instead of what we do. But God doesn't let our inadequacies keep his glory from being made known.

Journal

7

Your Invitation to Climb

Today is your day! Your mountain is waiting. So
. . . get on your way.

Dr. Seuss

I spent the afternoon and evening of my forty-sixth
birthday at Texas Children's Hospital in downtown
Houston. I sat in the crowded lab in the basement of the hospital after a very long day, thinking about the party I wasn't
having and feeling sorry for myself. It was the kind of self-
pity that isn't pretty. I thought that if people knew how I was
spending my birthday, they would feel sorry for me too—not
the party I imagined, but still a party.

A nurse interrupted my pity party to let me know the
two transplant patients (one heart, the other kidney) who
had just come in would need to step in front of us in line.
He explained that they were on a strict medicinal schedule
and the little guy who sat down next to me was due for a

dose and needed his blood drawn first. I nodded my head in agreement, and we settled in for another hour wait. Lunch had long been forgotten, and my stomach growled. After the nurse stepped back behind the closed doors, the parent of the boy next to me asked, pointing to my child, "Is yours a transplant kid too?"

I immediately snapped out of my self-absorbed thoughts and stumbled with my response, "Uh, oh, no. We are dealing with an eye disease . . ." My voice trailed off, and my words sounded foreign in my mouth. We had kept our child's condition private and still work toward anonymity, so this was the first time I shared the diagnosis with a stranger.

"I'm sorry to hear that," the dad responded. "Is there a cure?" I slowly shook my head no.

"Ah, only treatment, right? It's the treatment and side effects that keep us coming back here," he said with a note of bitterness. He pointed to his little boy and said, "He's on his second heart transplant, but this one is giving him trouble because the treatment also made him a Type 1 diabetic and has made his bones brittle. He will likely need another heart transplant in the next year." I was speechless. I was thankful my pity party had been private.

When the nurse called our new little acquaintance back for a blood draw, my child squeezed my hand reassuringly and whispered, "See? I'm thankful this is all I have."

When God said to let the little children lead us, maybe my child's beautiful display of wisdom is why. For the rest of the night, instead of self-pity, I felt only gratitude. It was the best kind of gift to unwrap on my birthday. Because sometimes the best way out of the darkness is by remembering and being thankful for all that you do have.

I believe one of the best places to be is out of our comfort zones, but they are also the most uncomfortable places because it shakes our security. We find security in what we know, in where we feel safe. But God will often turn our lives upside down because *he* wants to be our security. He isn't angry with us, and we haven't done anything wrong; he simply loves us too much to leave us stagnant. Many times, when God is trying to teach us something or take us deeper in our faith, he shakes our comfort and security, and for a while it feels dark, scary, and uncertain. But he is with us in the darkness, whispers *fear not* in our ears, takes our hand, and invites us to climb.

When we are talking about leaving what is comfortable and doing something hard—such as climbing a mountain we either dare to climb or must climb—what we are really discussing is obedience. This kind of obedience is brave. One of my favorite stories in the Bible is found in Luke 5:1–11. I have read this passage of Scripture countless times over the years and still draw much truth and wisdom from it.

> Once when he was standing on the shore of Lake Gennesaret, the crowd was pushing in on him to better hear the Word of God. He noticed two boats tied up. The fishermen had just left them and were out scrubbing their nets. He climbed into the boat that was Simon's and asked him to put out a little from the shore. Sitting there, using the boat for a pulpit, he taught the crowd.
>
> When he finished teaching, he said to Simon, "Push out into deep water and let your nets out for a catch."
>
> Simon said, "Master, we've been fishing hard all night and haven't caught even a minnow. But if you say so, I'll let out the nets." It was no sooner said than done—a huge haul

of fish, straining the nets past capacity. They waved to their partners in the other boat to come help them. They filled both boats, nearly swamping them with the catch.

Simon Peter, when he saw it, fell to his knees before Jesus. "Master, leave. I'm a sinner and can't handle this holiness. Leave me to myself." When they pulled in that catch of fish, awe overwhelmed Simon and everyone with him. It was the same with James and John, Zebedee's sons, coworkers with Simon.

Jesus said to Simon, "There is nothing to fear. From now on you'll be fishing for men and women." They pulled their boats up on the beach, left them, nets and all, and followed him. (Message)

In the past decade, God has taught me a lot about obedience. The following five lessons are worth sharing:

1. *Brave obedience starts with the Word.* The crowds were pressing in on Jesus to hear words from the Word. Jesus is the Word: "In the beginning was the Word, and the Word was with God and the Word was God. He was with God in the beginning" (John 1:1–2). He knows all things, and when he speaks, we gather round and press in to hear every word.

   Jesus spoke the Word of God with fishermen when he was fishing for men. People were with Jesus because power and authority were in the Word of God.

   We are good with words. We talk, we share, we offer advice—we say a lot. But it's too easy to just talk. That's what I did for years. There was a lot of faith and a lot of talking about God but very little action. There must be both—faith and obedience. One is not possible without the other.

2. *Brave obedience requires absolute trust.* In spite of Simon Peter's lack of faith, he trusted. Imagine fishing all night with no catch; it would be exhausting and discouraging. Yet at Jesus's word, he responded in action. Every time I read this story, I am amazed that Jesus was telling professional fishermen how to fish—and they listened! They had to trust his plan, not their own. Peter trusted and did what Jesus asked him to do despite how foolish it sounded.

3. *Brave obedience requires obedience.* It's a deep thought. We can get so good at being "Christians" that we become lazy and simply check off boxes. But we can't fake obedience or tick it off and think, *Well, I'm glad I'm done with that one.* Obedience is a way of life. It is obvious and evident in our lives, and there is fruit from our actions. Obedience can also bring fear or discomfort: "*At your word* I will let down the net" (NKJV, emphasis added).

4. *Brave obedience brings humility.* When we encounter God and see him do the impossible from the edge of our boat, our response glorifies God. When we meet Jesus face-to-face and recognize his holiness, we are reminded how great he is and how small we are. We can't take credit; his glory humbles us, points our lives to Jesus. We don't read that Peter said, "Look what I have done." No, he knows that the overwhelming catch was because he obeyed Jesus.

5. *Brave obedience produces a radical response.* When the fishermen had brought their boats to land, they left everything, including their catch, and followed

him. They leave the fish, the nets, the boats—everything—behind to follow Christ. There is a cost to wild obedience—it requires action.

Prepare

By the end of 2018, I was emotionally weary, financially depleted, spiritually empty, and physically exhausted, and my family was dragging itself into the new year. We decided to head to our favorite mountain getaway in New Mexico and jumped at the chance to take the eleven-hour road trip. But two days before we headed out, something unprecedented happened: the sky opened up and dumped forty-two inches of snow in twenty-four hours.

As we waited for the roads to reopen, we dug out puffy jackets, found missing gloves, and called about snow chains. We prepared for the journey. Doing anything less would have been careless and unwise because when you're changing your view, climbing new heights, and taking risks, you have to prepare for the adventure. Our spiritual journeys need the same consideration before we trek into the unknown. We need courage, tenacity, and wisdom for the mountains ahead. Mark Udall says, "You don't climb mountains without a team, you don't climb mountains without being fit, you don't climb mountains without being prepared, and you don't climb mountains without balancing the risks and rewards. And you never climb a mountain on accident—it has to be intentional."[1]

God doesn't dare us to dream or ask us to face an impossible mountain alone. He invites us. He equips us. He goes with us. James 1:5–7 says, "If any of you lacks wisdom, you should ask God, who gives generously to all without finding fault, and it will be given to you. But when you ask, you must believe and not doubt, because the one who doubts is like a wave of the sea, blown and tossed by the wind. That person should not expect to receive anything from the Lord."

When I read these verses, I think of faith. That's what we're really talking about, isn't it? Hebrews 11:1–2, the great faith chapter, tells us, "The fundamental fact of existence is that this trust in God, this faith, is the firm foundation under everything that makes life worth living. It's our handle on what we can't see" (Message). We will dig deeper into Hebrews 11 a little later, but we must understand that faith is what we hope will happen but don't presently see.

Name Your Mountain

There are all kinds of mountains in our lives. I didn't know that the last decade of climbing an impossible mountain like starting Mercy House would prepare me for overcoming the mountain of difficult family challenges. Although entirely different, they both have driven me to the feet of Jesus and made me desperate for him.

I believe God performs miracles. I've seen enough to know that he can do anything with anyone. When I'm tempted to forget what he can do, I just have to look behind me. The rearview mirror gives us a good view of just how far he can take us. I pray for the miracle of provision. I imagine thousand-dollar checks in the mail to make our job of fundraising a little easier. I pray for the miracle of healing—even when doctors say there is no cure. I ask the God who formed us, who knows every hair on our heads, to heal our brokenness. I ask. I believe. I expect.

On one of my trips to Kenya, I stood in a crowded room filled with precious women whose lives had been changed. They were sitting at looms and leaning over kilns. I have been an eyewitness to the impossible. I have watched God perform miracle after miracle. When God asked us to turn uneducated, mostly illiterate, often-hopeless poor women into skilled artisans, I knew it would take more miracles than we could muster. But when I stood on holy ground in that packed room filled with hope and testimony of how God had done more than we dreamed, I knew he was birthing a new dream: an artisan training center that would change more lives than we dreamed possible.

Just the thought made me want to run for the hills—and not the obedient kind of sprint. I live in a nearly constant state of being overwhelmed with my yes to God, so why would I keep saying it? What would entice me to go deeper and deeper over my head? It can only be because God often reveals his will by giving us dreams we didn't know we wanted and asking us to scale mountains we didn't think we could climb—he beckons because it's where his glory is revealed.

But it would be months and months before I was brave enough to say the words aloud. And when I did find the courage, it was at a Mercy House Global board retreat. I shared the vision, and I wept as I heard the impossibility of my own words. My friend Ann Voskamp, who sits on our board, clapped her hands and nodded her head, and other board members agreed that this was the direction God was leading. Within minutes, we were sharing audacious dreams and big ideas. My phone buzzed, and as the text message flashed across my screen, I sucked in a big gulp of air at the words and their uncanny timing. It was from my longtime friend and (in)courage cofounder Stephanie Bryant. She asked, "Are you praying about something big and/or new this year for Mercy House?"

I read the text aloud to our board of directors and stopped in the middle of the meeting to send this reply: "Here's a big (huge) dream: a vocational school in Kenya where we turn very poor women into skilled artisans."

We continued texting, and she didn't bat an eye at the large price tag that comes with such a dream. What I didn't know was that (in)courage and their parent company, Dayspring, owned by Hallmark, were behind her questions. They were interested in partnering with a nonprofit like Mercy House Global. We began a beautiful conversation that day and before the end of the year, (in)courage had raised $30,000 in our new partnership. Sometimes the first step in our climb is to state our dream out loud. We never know who might be listening. That first step began a domino effect that we are still chasing today.

Pray and Study the Word of God

In our hardest, darkest moments, God is there. He often uses hard things to break us so that his will and way can work out in our lives. John Eldredge writes, "Let's go ahead and name the elephant in the room: some prayers work, and some prayers don't. Why does that surprise and irritate us? . . . We want [prayer] to be simple and easy." But it's not. He goes on to say, "We want to pray; it's in our nature. We desperately want to believe that God will come through for us. But then, he doesn't seem to. . . . I believe he wants us to push through to real answers."[2]

When I think of my prayer life, I think of an ongoing conversation. I talk a lot; I share my complaints, my burdens, my dreams and fears. Some days there might be a little begging, other days, pure gratitude. It reminds me a little of parenting—this ongoing conversation we have with our kids who aren't afraid to ask us for what they want (sometimes over and over and over) and who sometimes forget to say thanks for what they've been given. My kids talk to me about everything—good and bad, highs and lows, and as they've gotten older, they try to tell me what to do too. See where I'm going? We do the same with our Father, and he is so patient with us. I think God wants us to share our thoughts and needs and dreams and desires in the same way. Eldredge challenges us with this truth: "Effective prayer is far more a partnership with God than it is begging him to do something."[3]

God wants the best for us just like we want the best for our kids. They don't always know what's best or how their decisions will impact their future. We correct and discipline them because of our great love for them. God does the same for us because he can see what we can't and is constantly working behind the scenes on our behalf. Luke 15:28–31 tells the story of the prodigal son's older brother. The father's explanation of his response to the homecoming of his wayward son reminds us that everything God has is ours for the asking.

Eldredge also writes:

Yes, yes—we have all heard that we are God's children; we are sons and daughters. The curse of familiarity with the words has dulled us to the staggering truth they contain.

The reality of it has not penetrated our hearts, not deeply enough. We still act and pray like orphans or slaves.

A slave feels reluctant to pray; they feel they have no right to ask, and so their prayers are modest and respectful. They spend more time asking forgiveness than they do praying for abundance. They view the relationship with reverence, maybe more like fear, but not with the tenderness of love. Of *being* loved. There is no intimacy in the language or their feelings. Sanctified unworthiness colors their view of prayer. These are often "good servants of the Lord."

An orphan is not reluctant to pray; they feel desperate. But their prayers feel more like begging than anything else. Orphans feel a great chasm between themselves and the One to whom they speak. Abundance is a foreign concept; a poverty mentality permeates their prayer lives. They ask for scraps; they expect scraps.

But not sons; sons know who they are.[4]

There have been many times in my parenting journey when I've longed for a how-to book with step-by-step instructions that would shed some light on the tough-to-navigate phases and challenges of raising kids. It would be a bestseller! But this is what the Bible is for believers. God, our Father, gave us this incredible guide for daily living, and it is alive and active and penetrates the broken and hardened places in our hearts. All we have to do is read it, which sadly is often our greatest challenge. You may be a lot like me—I struggle to make Bible reading a priority. When I do, I never regret the time I spend in the Word of God. It encourages, reminds, corrects, and inspires me again and again. It holds the answers my heart longs to hear.

Take Your Next Step

We've taken the first step and named our mountain; we've prayed and studied Scripture. What's next? It's time to lace up our hiking boots and do something. It doesn't have to be a giant leap; it can be a tiny baby step. Maybe it's confiding in a praying friend or writing down your thoughts in a notebook. Maybe it's making a phone call or setting up a meeting. It does not have to be big to be significant. God delights in our small yeses. I wrote about the many small yeses my life is made up of in *Rhinestone Jesus*. I never set out to help open three maternity homes in Kenya or to run an organization that sells millions of dollars in fair-trade product. I never dreamed this mountain climbing would lead to both my husband and me being employed by the nonprofit we began in our garage. To be honest, I'm so glad I didn't know. It would have terrified me to dangle from this high place, and I might have run the other way. God doesn't give us a ten-thousand-foot view for no reason. My desire was simply to help pregnant girls in Kenya, and all we are now doing still does that and so much more. God takes our simple yes, our offer of a lunch of five small loaves and two fish, and he does the impossible with it.

One thing is sure, we cannot climb alone. Think about adventure seekers who attempt crazy climbs and risky journeys—they don't do them alone. A friend of mine has made over one hundred jumps from an airplane and dives hundreds of feet underwater into caves (literally, a recurring nightmare for me), but she never does any of this alone. A solo climb could surely lead to accident or death; climbers climb in community. You should too.

Community often leads to collaboration, which eliminates competition. Sometimes we keep our dreams to ourselves because we don't want anyone to steal our ideas, but I believe when God gives us something to do, he wants us to lead others into unknown places as well. Leaders without followers are really just loners. Leaders have people following them (and not in the social media sense but in the Moses with a staff kind of way). God does the impossible with our simple yeses of obedience, but first we have to say it. Then we must act on it.

Worship While You Wait

Our church has been studying the book of Acts for over two years now, and we are only halfway through the book. It's a verse-by-verse study every Sunday. In many of the sermons, I have been inspired and challenged by the early church. Acts 13:1–12 is no exception. It's the story of Barnabas, Paul, a Jewish sorcerer, and the salvation of the governor of Paphos.

In this passage, we see that Barnabas and Paul were waiting on God to tell them what to do next. While they waited, they worshiped and fasted. What should we do when we don't know what to do next? We worship Jesus and we start with what we know.

I took notes on what my pastor said next: "God decides what we are called to do. He designed us to fulfill a role in the church, to live on mission. In these four men, we see diversity—racial, economic, spiritual, and even class. But God gives all of us gifts to build up the church. God calls all of us to move for the sake of the gospel. Some of us will be sent, most of us will stay, but none of us were made to sit. We are all called to serve."

Sitting is boring, unfulfilling, self-serving, and leads to a deeply unsatisfied life. We were made to climb, to risk, to do hard things. We were made for adventure. But while we wait for the next step, we still have something to do: worship. When we praise God for the known, we are also honoring the unknown. Worship invites others into our gratitude.

Nothing makes us feel alive like stepping into the unknown. When we take that first brave step in community and collaboration, we may just encourage others to do the same. We may just become part of a movement much bigger than we are. I believe God moves more mountains when we work together.

MOUNTAINTOP MOMENT

Oswald Chambers, an early twentieth-century evangelist, says, "We pray when there's nothing else we can do; Jesus wants us to pray before we do anything at all."[5]

We pray to our heavenly Father because we were created to fellowship with him. When we don't do what he created us to do, something is missing in our lives. It's this oneness with God, this fellowship and community, that brings us comfort, peace, and even joy in the highs and lows of this mountain-climbing life. He invites us to commune with him every step of the way.

1. Think about your devotional life for a minute. How can you make prayer an ongoing conversation?

2. Throughout your day, how can you return the invitation and invite God into your thoughts and activities? Try praying your way through your day.

3. For the past six months, I've been listening to an audio version of the Bible through the Bible app on my phone. Listening to "As It Happened," a chronological version of the Bible, has been enlightening and a page-turner. Try it!

Journal

8

Just Keep Climbing

Remember that guy that gave up? Neither does
anyone else.

Unknown

I missed the first deadline for this book. It was due in
the middle of our mess. But with doctor appointments and fund-raising for our Mercy House minicrisis, I
got behind on everything. But that's not the entire reason I
was late. I just didn't know what to say. I didn't know how
to keep climbing, and I certainly wasn't in a position to
encourage you to do so.

When I dug deep into my heart, I found two things: fear
and anger. I think the fear is understandable. But the anger
surprised me. I was mostly mad at God. I felt that he had
disappointed me on an unspoken deal I made with him: I'll
walk in brave obedience, and you keep my kids off-limits
from the enemy. We all know deals with God don't work,

but I had still made one, which made finding my way in the darkness even more difficult.

I did what we do in the darkness. I slowly and carefully, with arms outstretched and hands reaching, felt the way in front of me and took one small step at a time. I didn't quit. That first step is called hope. According to Anne Lamott, "Hope begins in the dark, the stubborn hope that if you just show up and try to do the right thing, the dawn will come. You wait and watch and work: you don't give up."[1]

Fear and Anger

You know this by now, but I would characterize myself as someone who is afraid of many things. You could say I'm scared of things that are out of my control—which covers a lot. And the more out of control I feel, the angrier I am. *Redbook* editor-in-chief Jill Herzig writes, "A wise therapist taught me that anger is the emotion we snatch up to avoid less comfortable feelings—confusion, fear, sadness."[2]

Being afraid for your child and a little angry about what they are going through heightens both emotions to a whole new level. On one of our many trips to the hospital in the past few months, we stopped to visit with a sweet little girl who was on her sixty-something day in the hospital. I met her mom when I was speaking at a church in my hometown. She and her husband served there as youth pastors.

Mercy House Global had set up a pop-up shop at their church, and I was helping at one of the tables when she walked up to me, holding one of my books, and said, "Is this the same Kristen Welch who started Mercy House?" I smiled as we talked about me in the third person for a few seconds, and then I told her I had written the book she was holding.

As we chatted, I learned that she had the night off from hospital duty where her little girl, who had been diagnosed with aplastic anemia, was living and waiting on a bone marrow match. She was too sick to go home. Her mountain made my knees weak. I saw a little bit of fear in her eyes as she talked about the unknown, and I heard a dab of anger in her words as she talked about fighting for her girl. We realized our kids were being treated at the same hospital, and we planned to visit the next time we were in the same place.

A couple of weeks later, she invited us into her daughter's sterile world. Before I entered her hospital room, I was afraid. I was terrified of the unknown for my child, for the side effects I couldn't control, and for a disease I didn't know how to beat. But all that fear was forgotten as I watched my healthy child, by comparison, bend down to help unwrap a new toy and play with her tiny sick child.

I have said it so often I ought to have it tattooed: perspective changes everything. Suffering is something the Lord promises throughout the Bible that we will have to endure. There will be suffering in this life. But as I sat next to my new friend, both of us watching our kids closely, I felt less alone. We didn't need to compare our suffering; we found comfort being together in the middle of it.

We don't climb alone. We may often feel alone, but when we are vulnerable and share our struggles, we discover others on the same road. It is true that God is with us, and he is enough. But in his goodness, he sends a host of other people who come alongside and lift our arms when they are too tired, restock our supplies when we are empty, and stand on the edge chanting, "*Don't give up.*"

When I googled how many times the Bible says "Fear not," dozens of links popped up saying it's recorded 365 times—one for every day of the year. While I'm not certain of the accuracy of this number, I did love the enthusiasm. It reinforces the truth I've discovered: fear is a part of life. The Bible doesn't repeatedly ask, "Why are you afraid?" That feels a little judgmental, and besides, we all know the answer—life can be very scary. Instead, it says in so many words, "Girl, I know you're afraid. But don't be, because I'm with you. You are not alone on the mountain. I've got this."

In her book *Fear and Faith*, Trillia Newbell says, "We don't want to wait until our fears come true. We want to prepare now."[3] In an interview with Trillia, Thomas Bowen, a writer at Radical.net, asked her, "How do you prepare?" Trillia said:

> We prepare by studying God's Word, learning about his character, and rehearsing the gospel to our hearts. . . . We learn to love God above all else. . . . When our fears do come true and we experience death, for example, we remember truths like death's sting will cease and that we have a living hope.[4]

When I read these encouraging words, I thought of 1 John 4:16–19:

> We have come to know and to believe the love that God has for us. God is love, and whoever abides in love abides in God, and God abides in him. By this is love perfected with us, so that we may have confidence for the day of judgment, because as he is so also are we in this world. There is no fear

in love, but perfect love casts out fear. For fear has to do with punishment, and whoever fears has not been perfected in love. We love because he first loved us. (ESV)

Thomas Bowen pressed Trillia further and asked, "You talk about combating all our earthly, sinful fears by fearing God. What does this look like?" She replied:

To combat fear by fearing God is to first know God through his word. . . . I ask God to give me faith to believe. . . . I ask him to continue to teach me about himself so that I might grow in love with him. In the end, I think as we do this we also grow in the fear of the Lord.[5]

What happened in that hospital room has happened a thousand times. I was afraid in the darkness, but as Mosaic Church declares in their song "Tremble": "Jesus, Jesus, You make the darkness tremble . . . You silence fear."[6] With his great love for me and my trust in him, he quieted my fear.

When You Are the Mountain in the Way

Have you heard the song "Rescue" by Lauren Daigle? A friend who went with me on a trip to Kenya sent me a link to the song after it came out and said every time she heard it, she was reminded of the teen moms in Kenya who captured my heart more than a decade ago. But the more I listened to it, I realized it was written for me too. Because sometimes as you are climbing a challenging and overwhelming mountain, you just need to be reminded that you're not lost in the darkness. Or if you are lost, that God will send out an army to find you in the middle of the darkest night. He says, *I will rescue you.* More than once, I had to stop writing and dry my eyes because the words found their mark. But don't take my word for it; listen to Lauren belt it a few times—or a few hundred—and I promise it will encourage you too.

Mountain climbers call the area above 26,247 feet on Mount Everest the "death zone" because there is not enough oxygen for people to breathe, causing them to become weak and struggle to think straight and make decisions. In fact, "Most of the 200+ climbers who have died on Mount Everest have died in the death zone. Due to the inverse relationship of atmospheric pressure to altitude, at the top of Mount Everest the average person takes in about 30% of the oxygen in the air that they would take in at sea level; a human used to breathing air at sea level could only be there for a few minutes before they became unconscious."[7] Most climbers carry oxygen bottles in order to make it to the top.

I don't know about you, but I have no plans to ever climb Mount Everest. But that doesn't mean I don't know something about the death zone—the metaphorical space where it's hard to breathe, where I feel weak and can't think straight and struggle to make decisions. Can anyone else relate? When I have faced adversity, I have gasped and clawed for a deep breath. Today, at this exact moment, I'm breathless from the climb, and in the most vulnerable way I can say it, I want off this mountain. But as much as I want God to miraculously move it out of my way, he has not. He is showing me that the best way around the mountain is through it.

When I was a kid, my dad challenged my sister and me to memorize the first chapter of James. I loved a good challenge, and so I accepted it. I've never regretted it. These powerful verses come to mind whenever I need them most:

Consider it pure joy, my brothers and sisters, whenever you face trials of many kinds, because you know that the testing of your faith produces perseverance. Let perseverance finish its work so that you may be mature and complete, not lacking anything. If any of you lacks wisdom, you should ask God, who gives generously to all without finding fault, and it will be given to you. But when you ask, you must believe and not doubt, because the one who doubts is like a wave of the sea, blown and tossed by the wind. That person should not expect to receive anything from the Lord. Such a person is double-minded and unstable in all they do. (James 1:2–8)

My Lifeway Women's Study Bible says, "Adversity is not God's ultimate desire for his creation; yet, there is a clear message that God uses adversity. He is in control over the most adverse circumstances."[8] God often keeps the circumstances the same. He doesn't move the mountains—he moves us. He asks us to go through the mountains to overcome them.

In *Raising World Changers*, I wrote about one of our favorite mountainous spots to visit—Gunnison, Colorado. We even named our eighty-pound Sheepadoodle Gunnison after the beautiful town. One of our favorite places to eat in the area is the Sherpa Café run by a kind Nepali family. Their delicious blend of Nepali and Indian food has had us trying to replicate recipes. It's also piqued our interest to learn more about Sherpas. We learned that they are a small Nepalese ethnic group renowned for their incredible climbing skills in very high altitudes, often at a very high risk to their lives. "Sherpas act as guides and porters, and do everything from carrying the loads to setting up the camps. They secure climbing routes, fix lines, ferry supplies and guide clients to the top of Everest and other Himalayan peaks."[9]

The café has pictures on the walls of Sherpas doing just that. On one of our visits, I remember thinking (1) I would never do that, and (2) but if I did, I would trust the Sherpa. These guides lead the way in harsh, even blinding, circumstances when you can't see your hand in front of your face due to wind, snow, and ice pelting you. They stand between a successful climb and a need for rescue. We often think of the need for rescue in terms of someone who is at the mercy of someone else. But this climb I'm on has caused me to discover that I mostly need to be rescued from me.

When some friends invited our family to their Houston home one night for homemade Indian food, I had no idea the blessing that was waiting for me. I did know that Terrell and I would finally get to meet some mutual friends, a couple who led a nonprofit in India similar to Mercy House Global, whom we had known only through email. They were longtime missionaries in India and had recently come back to the United States. We met and collaborated in our work to empower women. As soon as our family walked in the door, Mala and I moved to a corner of the room so we could talk quietly. It's always amazing how God connects us with people with similar missions and the same brave obedience to fulfill them. Within minutes, she had zeroed in on my messy heart. I didn't share anything we were going through personally or the heaviness of Mercy House, but she sensed the stress, and I think she recognized herself in my weariness.

She did something I desperately needed but didn't know how to ask for: she spoke to the exhausted leader in me as someone who had been there herself. She told me where the track I was on would lead, and she gave me permission to get off it. She spoke openly of her own breakdown and said in a prophetic hushed whisper, "Kristen, if you don't slow down and change how hard you're working, you won't quit because you want to; you'll quit because you *have* to."

At first, I objected. I defended the work, my involvement, my weariness, and how badly Mercy House needed me to give 150 percent all the time. I told her how even when I take a day off, I return to answer questions and help solve problems. "I don't know how to change it," I said, my voice breaking. The more we talked, the more I realized the mountain in my way was me, the accidental nonprofit founder lost in the darkness on a big scary mountain. Her words were direct and holy, and I devoured them.

We continued to talk throughout dinner and dessert, and I was desperate for more direction from someone who had learned what I was still studying. She said, "Do you know what to do when your staff asks you questions? You don't answer them; instead, you ask, 'How would you solve this problem?' Nine times out of ten they have the answer but are afraid to do it on their own because they don't want to let you down." We talked about being leaders and moms and how very difficult it is to do both well. She confessed some regret, and her words sounded an alarm in my brain. My kids haven't always gotten the best of me, and all I could think about was this new diagnosis and how they needed me present more than ever. All of a sudden, I had clarity. I decided right then and there to get out of the way. I knew there was no question about what I should do or where I should be. Mala had shared a dozen life-giving tidbits of wisdom, and I cried the whole way home.

The next day, I gathered my staff around to tell them I would be making some changes because my family needed me. I said that I needed to trust them more and had decided to let them solve some of the day-to-day issues. We would weather together any mistakes made. They weren't nervous; in fact, they seemed almost relieved. Because maybe I was a mountain in *their* way too. I announced I would be in the office only two or three days a week for the foreseeable future. These immediate changes breathed life, creativity, and energy back into me like nothing had in years. With more room to breathe at work, I continued to climb.

I was scrolling through Facebook one day as one does, and I stopped when I read these words by Ann Voskamp:

> There's a whole bunch of us marching along private battles nobody knows about, climbing hard mountains that nobody sees, wrestling tough things that nobody has any idea about. Maybe you need to hear this too? You're not alone: He sees you.
>
> So you simply purpose to pray, and simply pray for perseverance—today's your very own clean slate of fresh possibilities—pray, persevere, do your hard & holy things. . . .
>
> But this is all that ever matters: God always sees and He will always see to the matter. . . .
>
> And He is always there with you.[10]

MOUNTAINTOP MOMENT

There is likely going to come a day when you want to quit—that crisis, that class, that calling, that kid. When that day arrives, you have to stand on the mountain of your mess and remember that quitting isn't the solution—but surrendering is. Maybe you want to give up on your marriage, your mission, your motherhood. Friend, you can't give it up, but you can give it over to God. Maybe you are carrying something heavy that isn't yours to bear—the blame for your broken marriage, the burden of your wayward child, the brokenness of this life. I love these words from Mary Anne Radmacher: "Courage doesn't always roar. Sometimes courage is the quiet voice at the end of the day saying (whispering), I will try again tomorrow."[11]

1. Be honest and think through what quitting would accomplish. Sometimes the best way to attack the fear that besets us is to picture the worst. In our imagining, we can still see Jesus in the middle of it.

2. Surrender requires the discipline of laying down our burdens and refusing to pick them back up. What does surrender look like?

3. Who are the Sherpas in your life, leading and guiding you over the mountain?

Journal

9

Rainbows in the Rain

For nothing will be impossible with God.

Luke 1:37 (ESV)

My favorite kind of day isn't a sunny one. I live in Houston, and we are known for our hot, humid weather. But I don't love a wet day either. We have experienced record amounts of rain in the past few years. Because our temperatures can go from hot to brutal in a matter of hours, I appreciate the milder temperatures a good rain brings. But I don't want it to rain all day. When it does, I want to lie in bed under the covers, eat Chinese food, and binge on Netflix. It's my thing.

The days I love best are a mix of rain and sun—just enough rain to cool things down but not soak the grass. On these days, rainbows are most likely to peek from behind the clouds, and they remind me that there is always, always something to be thankful for. This thought has permeated my heart and mind for the last decade. No matter what I have faced, our ministry has endured, or my family has overcome, there is always something to thank God for—these little moments are magnificent rays that reveal him in the middle of the rain.

In the very rough season we were in, there were also rainbows. These precious moments included sending our oldest to college, watching our tender, six-foot son come into his own, and sweet memories of our youngest taking more steps of independence. There was another long-awaited rainbow that burst through the clouds as well; it was life giving for our family.

For as long as we've been married (over twenty-five years now), Terrell has had a dream to own a rental property. He's read real estate articles and books, listened to podcasts and audiobooks, and dreamed. He is incredibly handy, the kind of guy who can fix anything or build whatever I see on Pinterest—a true renovator at heart. Somewhere along the way, as is often the case in a marriage, his dream became mine. I have the business sense of a fig, so it didn't appeal to me at all, but I wanted my faithful, hardworking husband to see his dream come true because I love him.

Like the average family, we could never quite save enough for a down payment or finagle enough money out of our budget to put away toward this dream. Yet we still hoped because that's what dreams will do to you—they dare you to reach for the impossible. But this wasn't merely a business idea to bring in extra income for when our kids were preparing for or attending college. We also longed for a place we could escape to.

As I mentioned earlier, we live in the neighborhood behind Mercy House Global. The red barn is just a few steps away and houses our largest retail store, shipping warehouse, and offices. It's close and convenient but really hard to get away from. Even with strict office hours and boundaries in place, it seems there is a reason every day of the week we need to be at the barn—whether it's a backed-up sewage system, which sadly happens more often than anyone with a strong sense of smell would want, or an out-of-town shopper who traveled hours and really just wants to hug you. And this doesn't include the many nights we lie in bed working out some new challenge. I like to call the barn a vacuum—it sucks you in, and it's hard to get out. This is great when we need volunteers and shoppers, but it sort of backfires when you're burned out and need a day at home to recuperate.

If you ever come to visit, serve, or shop (which you *should*), you will see the shelves, counters, and one-of-a-kind displays that Terrell made by hand. He loves doing projects like these because there's an end to the job. You can hammer in the last nail, stand back, and see that you've accomplished something. When your day job is to fund the rescues of pregnant teens, empower their families with dignified jobs, and redeem future generations, success or "finished projects" aren't defined as easily.

Something unexpected happened that brought us a little closer to making our dream of rental property come true—I got a royalty check in the mail. The first time this happened, I asked God if the extra money was a blessing or a test. Even as I asked it, I knew it was a test—one I really wanted to pass. We donated that money, and we've never regretted it.

I passed that test but have failed many others. I spent a big chunk of my life seeing extra provision as a blessing for me and my family so that we could have more. But the more

I got, the emptier I felt. When we started sharing what we'd been given, we discovered true joy: it is better to give than to receive.

When a second royalty check came in for about the same amount we'd previously given away, I asked the same question. This time, I had peace about putting it toward our longtime dream. We had very few requirements when it came to owning a rental property: (1) It had to be in the mountains and in a place Airbnb considered highly rentable. (2) It had to be within a day's drive from our front door. (3) It had to be in a price range such that we could put down a deposit and have payments covered by rentals. (4) It had to be a fixer-upper (which was obvious considering our budget). Easy, right?

Even when our dream wasn't possible, we narrowed down cities and drove around for days and, well, dreamed. This was a risk we were itching to take, a mountain we wanted to climb, but like most dreams, there were days it seemed matching all our criteria was impossible.

At the end of December 2017, the itch needed to be scratched. We decided to drive to the nearest mountain town in New Mexico for a couple of days of rest and planned to spend a day looking at condos with a realtor friend who lived in the area. Terrell was getting sleepy on the drive, so on a whim, I bought the audio version of Chip Gaines's new book, *Capital Gaines*, and played it for the car ride. We are Texans, so we are very familiar with Magnolia Market and the Gaines empire, and we are fans. At first, my kids whined about a boring book, but after listening to Chip read the first chapter in his funny, casual way, they were asking us to turn it up.

We loved the book. And it was timely, considering the number of pages lying on the dashboard of condo units on the market we wanted to visit. How could we not follow our dream with Chip's words ringing in our ears:

> If there's something stirring in you now, and you know what it is, do that. There's no need to overthink it. A mistake here and there isn't going to kill you, so don't waste time worrying about that. It's infinitely better to fail with courage than to sit idle with fear, because only one of these gives you the slightest chance to live abundantly. And if you do fail, then the worst-case scenario is that you'll learn something from it. You're for sure not going to learn jack squat from sitting still and playing it safe. And challenges like "Not one of us is getting any younger" and waiting for your "perfect moment" or for the "most convenient time" could very well turn into a missed opportunity.[1]

By the time we finished the audiobook, we were pulling in to the place we were staying in New Mexico. We were exhausted but exhilarated. We were ready to climb.

As I write this, only a handful of people know that we own an Airbnb in New Mexico. It has been this secret place we run to for rest and renewal whenever we can. During our sabbatical, we spent weeks ripping out walls and painting doors and getting our hands dirty. Late one night, we even superglued closed a gash in Terrell's leg. It became a holy place where we got away from what we do and, in some ways, who people think we are. No one knows us or expects anything from us. But it was a huge risk for us financially, so we worked our tails off to get it ready to rent. I'm happy to report it has been booked every weekend since we listed it. It's not making us rich, but we are able to apply a little bit toward college tuition each month.

It had been six months since we had last made the long drive to New Mexico due to the unforeseen adventures and hardships, and we were crawling toward rest. We knew the condo needed to be restocked with toilet paper and trash bags, and we needed to make a couple of repairs, so we snuck away to the mountains when the condo was vacant. As I lay in bed in this home away from home, I thought about what a blessing this tiny oasis had become during one of the most difficult years of our lives. It was a rainbow in the rain.

Early the next morning, after an amazing night of sleep, I turned to Terrell and said, "I think I should write about this place in my book. It's a dream come true. It's a mountain we chose to climb. This place that we dreamed of for so long is a happy place in the middle of the storm." He agreed, both of us thinking about the scary mountains that still loomed large.

I wanted to let you in on this secret so that you will remember to pursue your dreams even if you are living a nightmare. I wanted to encourage you to look for the rainbows in the rain. They are a reminder that God remembers his promise to us and that there can be good in the bad, joy in the sorrow. They remind us that God delights in doing the impossible. Nothing is impossible for him. What can God do exactly? Anything. Why does he do it in this way? I have no idea. But I believe him when he says it will work out for our good.

I told you a few chapters back about my layover in Germany between trips to Israel and Kenya. It was my fourth trip to Africa in 2018, and I was running on fumes. But every trip is a gift I get to unwrap, a search for the lesson I know God wants to teach me, an opportunity for him to redeem a little more of the brokenness in me. It happened in the home of a woman named Mary. We had walked the very precarious and slippery path to the bottom of Mathare slum, the same slum where my heart was split wide open on my first trip to Kenya in 2010 with Compassion International. In my book *Rhinestone Jesus*, this is how I described my surroundings on that first trip:

> Armed guards walked me, a group of other bloggers, and our guides down a muddy trail into Mathare Valley, one of Kenya's largest slums and most dangerous areas. We were observing and writing on behalf of Compassion International, who had arranged the trip.
>
> I trembled from more than fear. There was hopelessness everywhere I looked—endless tiny tin shanties where hundreds of thousands of people were crowded, "homes" with no electricity or running water. Plastic bags full of sewage floated in a green stream, and the ground wasn't made of dirt at all—it was just a mountain of trampled garbage. The stench nearly gagged me.
>
> A majority of the residents were small, unsupervised children. They called out to us, "How-ah-you? How-ah-you?" hoping we would put something into their upturned hands. We could see by their swollen bellies that they were malnourished. Their faces were filthy and covered with flies, which they didn't bother to shoo away.
>
> It was a hellhole, not fit for the living.[2]

When we got to Mary's home, there was a massive river of sewage and trash flowing across from her front door. It was impossible to ignore the raging sound and putrid smell. Our group from Mercy House crowded into her home, and she welcomed us with a proud smile. It was the first home she had ever rented, with its flimsy plastic walls and fragile roof, and she was proud to have guests.

Mary immediately stood on one foot, thrusting both arms out to either side, and then she switched feet. We all looked at one another and didn't know what to say about her strange welcome. Maureen, our director and local hero of Mercy House Global's work in Kenya, explained that Mary was showing us she was sober. I had met Mary for the first time three years before and that alone was a miracle, as I recalled her menacing behavior while high on glue. Many street moms sniff it to dull their aching hunger pains.

Mary gave us the quick tour of her one room that was about the size of a walk-in closet back home. She was a part of Street Hope, the artisan group we started at Mercy House Global that provided dignified jobs for former street moms who begged and prostituted themselves for survival.

"Mary, did you think a year ago you'd have a sewing job? How has it improved your life?" I asked.

She looked me in the eye and said, "I was born to be a beggar. My fate has always been to suffer. That's all I knew." She paused for a long time, and then smiled big. "But then I got a job sewing felt and moved into my first house, and one day I'll have a TV. This job has changed everything."

As we sat in her home, we talked about how impossible it was to dream of a better life when you can't even imagine it, when a river of sewage is your only view.

Maureen said later, "I dream of taking the sixteen women in Mary's group to a fine hotel and letting them sleep in a luxurious bed for the first time, experience a hot shower, be served delicious food. I want to give them something to dream about—something more than survival for the day or week."

My first thought was that it was impossible. A weekend like that would cost thousands of dollars—just getting them there would be a challenge. But I had a donor with me on that trip, and when she heard those words, she said, "Tell me how much that would cost. I want to see this dream come true." Once again, and more times than I can count, I was reminded that nothing is impossible with God.

The next month, Mary's group, sixteen of the women who make up Street Hope, walked into a fine hotel for a weekend retreat. I sat on my couch and sobbed when I read Mary's words about her weekend:

> I can afford to put on a big smile because I brushed my teeth for the first time today since I joined this world. I also smell so nice; thanks to the perfumed roll-ons I was given. The first time I stepped into this hotel, I didn't know what I was expected to do. I remember filling up my plate with all kinds of food. I ate to my fill, and I am so happy that I don't have to pay a single dime to have enjoyed all this. . . . I have never been loved before and I have always been looked down upon because of being considered a street urchin. Since I joined Street Hope, I have been loved so much and considered a human being. Thanks for showing me that indeed I matter in the eyes of the Lord regardless of my situation. I owe God my life, and I thank him for promising me that he will do great exploits, using my story and my life.

For the first time in their lives, these brave women stayed in a hotel, slept on clean sheets, enjoyed a hot shower, and filled their plates from a large buffet. Basically, they experienced what we take for granted every day. And do you know what happened? Exactly what we hoped: they stood a little taller, used their best manners, and began to dream things they never thought possible.

The amazing thing is God does this for each of us. Back in Mary's house with my staff that day, after she'd answered a few of our questions, I was speechless when one of my quieter staff members addressed Mary. "May I tell you my story?" she asked. This employee has worked behind the scenes at Mercy House Global for a couple of years. She is reserved, very detail-oriented, and extremely disciplined. This was her first trip to Kenya. I leaned in because I wanted to hear more of her story too.

"Mary, a couple years ago, I was living in my town, and I had a nice house and car and everything I needed. But some days I didn't want to get out of bed. I was sad and depressed, and I took medicine to feel better. But then I started working at Mercy House and learned about women like you. One of my jobs was to help sell and ship what you make. Mary, I want you to know that I can't wait to get up every day. Thank you."

This was it—God's gift, the lesson he had for me, the words I needed to hear. Everything about the moment screamed impossibilities—that an uneducated, medically fragile, illiterate woman who was a former homeless addict would provide purpose and meaning for a middle-class American woman. But Galatians 5:6 tells us, "For when we place our faith in Christ Jesus, there is no benefit in being circumcised or being uncircumcised. What is important is faith expressing itself in love" (NLT). This is what God does—the impossible.

Friends, this is life—a mix of good and bad, happy and sad, storms and sunshine. Life is a mixture of beauty and sadness—rainbows in the rain. I do love a good story. I see God in stories. I love writing and telling stories. But I prefer happy endings. I always choose movies or books that have a happy ending. If I could, I would write happy endings for the women in Kenya so they wouldn't have to beg or prostitute themselves, and for my children so they wouldn't have to face suffering. But as we know, life doesn't always give us that choice.

One of my greatest struggles in writing this book has been that I don't have a tidy ending. I can't look back on the past year and say, Oh, there's the redemption. Seasons in our lives don't always have a neatly tied bow around them. They can be messy and hard and dark. And today, right now, that's where I am—in the darkness, in the rain, waiting for the rainbow to peek from behind the clouds.

As I was contemplating my topsy-turvy life, I received some long-awaited (good) answers to some big questions I'd asked a few people I love and respect. We were planning a first-ever webcast at Mercy House that would focus on the theology of justice for the poor and the practicality of providing it through fair trade. I had invited Ann Voskamp, Myquillyn Smith (The Nester), Shaun Groves, Jen Schmidt, and Maureen Kaderi—a collection of mighty world changers—to participate, and within a week all of them accepted.

I was thrilled with the news, so overwhelmed, in fact, that I let out a rare whoop! I threw my hands in the air and loudly said to my staff, "If Jesus came back right now, I would feel that I had accomplished something with my life." I'm sure I scared some people, but I'm at that point in my life (maybe this happens to everyone at forty-six) when I'm mostly confident in myself and don't need to be validated.

But when people you love and respect want to be a part of a dream you have, it does just that. More than once, I thought, *Today is a good day.*

Four hours later, I was sitting on my bed at home, poring over unpaid medical bills, worried about meeting Mercy House's budget another year, angry with God (and just about everyone in my path) about the unexpected medical condition and before I knew it, I was crying into my pillow, thinking, *Jesus, come back so I don't have to deal with any of this anymore,* and then this thought, *Today is rough.*

If I hadn't been feeling so sorry for myself, I would have laughed at my emotional extremes within just a few hours of each other: fearless and afraid; full of faith and completely lacking it; daring to dream and wishing I'd never gotten out of bed that morning. It's not pretty, but it's the truth—this is me. I lead with a limp. I'm the unlikely, introverted mom who started a nonprofit and who still doubts a miracle-working Savior.

One minute I feel as if I am just getting started on this journey with God, and I am full of audacious plans; the next minute I'm angry at him for getting me into this mess. Is that too honest? Maybe, but it's the truth. More often than not, my days turn out to be two-steps-forward-and-one-step-backward kinds of days.

MOUNTAINTOP MOMENT

Even with all the crazy switchbacks and backtracking, we are getting somewhere. Growth isn't always linear. That night, I had a good cry and took a hot bath with the giant bath bomb I had been saving for a rainy day. I felt a bit sorry for myself and cursed the mountains still looming over me; then I dried my tears and gave myself the following pep talk. Maybe you need to hear it too.

Pull it together, girl. Enjoy the steps forward—revel in them for a minute. You worked hard; you did well. Give yourself a moment to cry over today's setback—go ahead, lick your wounds, but don't let it turn into tomorrow's fear.

Now do the math: two minus one is one. That is still something. It's all in the way you look at it. Two steps forward and one step backward isn't failure; it's a cha-cha or what we call the Texas Two-Step. Your missteps might just encourage someone else. So hush and dance. Sometimes turning those two-steps-forward-and-one-step-backward days into a dance is just a matter of perspective. It's also a reminder that nothing is impossible for God.

1. Write down a dream you have. Go wild; make it an impossible one.
2. How can you look for the rainbows in the middle of the rain? Is this something that comes easily for you?
3. Write a pep talk to yourself to pull out on a rainy day.

Journal

10

Miracle Territory

The miracle is not that we do this work but that we are happy to do it.

Mother Teresa

One night, too late to be awake, I turned to Terrell and said, "Are you still up?" When I felt his nod, I said, "I just need to say something out loud." I paused and he waited, and I took a deep breath. "I want an easy year."

He turned toward me, and I could feel his unasked question hanging in the air.

A few hours earlier we had been talking about the current needs at Mercy House as we started a new year. We had our own personal needs too. It was a depressing conversation because we didn't know how to meet either. We needed more miracles. We didn't solve any problems, and at some point, we simply stopped talking about it. But as I lay in bed some

151

time later, I couldn't sleep, and I just needed to say the one thing I hadn't, the one thing I shouldn't.

"Every year for as long as I can remember in the pursuit of this dream, there has been a disaster, a death, a dire need, or a diagnosis. I just want to have one year that's easy—a year to glide and catch our breath, a windfall year when we don't have to worry about raising money for Mercy House because it's miraculously taken care of, a year with no unexpected bills, a season without mountains to overcome. I want an easy year like . . ." As my words trailed off, a tear slipped onto my pillow.

He was quiet for a long time. I knew he didn't know what to do with my raw words, which sounded so selfish, self-centered, and painfully honest. He very quietly and tenderly touched my hand, and I knew he wouldn't say a word. But I needed him to do more than hear me; I wanted my vulnerability to be validated. And so I said more. I reminded him of every mountain we had faced and of the ones that loomed larger than ever in the darkness. I sounded sort of pathetic as I recounted the battle wounds.

"Honey, I love you. You sound burned out." I bristled at his words because I thought I had taken the right steps *not* to burn out. In an effort to be vulnerable, I felt misunderstood. I have this continual, strong drive to do more, to solve impossible problems, to change the world. When I imagine walking away from this difficult dream called Mercy House, my next image is of me starting something else like it among refugees in my city. I pressed him to say more, and he did.

"Honey, I feel the exact opposite. Think about how easy our lives are compared to the women in poverty whom we work to empower. I think God uses these hardships to teach us lessons we can't learn any other way," he whispered. Ah, a dagger. Even though it was wielded as tenderly as possible.

"I *am* thinking about those women. That's why it's so painful to say this out loud. For the last decade, I've spent most of my waking moments thinking about what I can do to ease their pain and change their situations. And I guess I want to be rewarded for that with a windfall year in which God says, *She deserves an easy season*." I hated the words that came out of my mouth because I knew this wasn't the gospel. This was all me.

I think my cry for an easy season was also a cry for rest. You might have gathered by now that I'm not good at resting. When our staff at Mercy House took the StrengthFinders test collectively, I was amazed at how helpful the results were in understanding not only coworkers but also myself. Four of my five strengths were centered on accomplishing (tasks) rather than being (relationally with people).

I'm a habitual striver. I don't rest even when I'm sleeping. I'm constantly solving problems in my head. It can be amazing because the results feed my strengths, but it's also exhausting.

When I read these words from Priscilla Shirer, I was so convicted: "Overwork is a form of unbelief."[1] When I succumb to working too much, I'm also not trusting God.

I thought about how I sometimes have this overwhelming urge to quit this mountain I'm on, to pack up and head back down the mountain as quickly as I can. Maybe this feeling isn't just momentary selfishness, fear, or exhaustion. Maybe it's urging from the Holy Spirit to stop striving, stop doing, stop fixing, and instead surrender. I'm learning that the space between striving and surrender looks like Sabbath.

This internal battle sets me on fire. I long for comfort but need discomfort to accomplish what is before me; I compare myself to people who have more rather than people who have less; I see the two-steps-forward-and-one-step-backward day as a setback instead of a salsa. But Terrell was right. I don't know if he heard me when I whispered back, "Yes, I feel burned out from purpose; I am burning with passion."

He held me as I cried because his words and validation couldn't calm the inner storm that God uses to whittle away things in me that are in the way. He was removing what wasn't necessary. He saw my limp and beckoned me to lead in spite of it. I knew in my gut God was toiling the earth of my heart, removing the rocks, pulling the weeds. He was preparing the ground for a miracle. Christine Caine, justice activist and author, says, "Impossible is where God starts. Miracles are what God does."[2]

If I've learned anything while chasing this dream and dodging disaster along the way, it's this: on the precipice of every miracle, there is a desperate need for Jesus. I don't use the word *miracle* lightly. How can I when the definition is "an extraordinary event manifesting divine intervention in human affairs; an extremely outstanding or unusual event, thing, or accomplishment"?[3] Miracles are rare, and yet they have become a regular part of my life at Mercy House Global. We have had more holy-ground moments of unexpected divine interventions than I can recount—from fifty miracle rescues to fifty miracle births, to miracles in my marriage, to God providing financial blessings in the nick of time. Yes, I believe in miracles. Not only do I believe that God does the impossible, but I also ask him to do the impossible on a regular basis.

But before there is a miracle, there is a measure of faith. Faith precedes the miracle. Romans 12:3 says, "Do not think of yourself more highly than you ought, but rather think of yourself with sober judgment, in accordance with the faith God has distributed to each of you."

This comes on the heels of my two favorite verses in the entire Bible, and I love how they read in the Message:

> So here's what I want you to do, God helping you: Take your everyday, ordinary life—your sleeping, eating, going-to-work, and walking-around life—and place it before God as an offering. Embracing what God does for you is the best thing you can do for him. Don't become so well-adjusted to your culture that you fit into it without even thinking. Instead, fix your attention on God. You'll be changed from the inside out. Readily recognize what he wants from you, and quickly respond to it. Unlike the culture around you, always dragging you down to its level of immaturity, God brings the best out of you, develops well-formed maturity in you. (Rom. 12:1–2)

I love that after Paul gives us specific instructions for how to live and dream in verses 1–2, he brings us back to reality in verse 3 and reminds us that we aren't much without Jesus. We can't move mountains without him. So how is faith measured?

Pastor and author John Piper says:

> God has given all Christians varying measures of faith. This is the faith with which we receive and use our varying gifts. It is the ordinary daily faith by which we live and minister. In the context, Paul is concerned that people were "thinking of themselves more highly than they ought to think." His

final remedy for this pride is to say that not only are spiritual gifts a work of God's free grace in our lives, but so also is the very faith with which we use those gifts. This means that every possible ground of boasting is taken away. How can we boast if even the qualification for receiving gifts is also a gift?

That's how important humility is in God's eyes. This is exactly the same aim of God mentioned in Ephesians 2:8–9 where Paul stresses that saving faith is a gift: "By grace you have been saved through faith; and that not of yourselves, it is the gift of God; not of works, so that no one may boast." Faith is a gift from God, so that no one may boast.[4]

When I think of someone who was more fearful than brave—but with a measure of faith—and who definitely didn't boast of his abilities, I think of Gideon. When I was in Israel, one of our stops was at Ein Harod, the spring of Gideon, written about in Judges 7. I love this story. It is an important one for us to consider, and it has been incredibly encouraging.

Gideon was a military leader who was also a prophet and a judge. In verse 2, God says to Gideon, "You have too many men. I cannot deliver Midian into their hands, or Israel would boast against me, 'My own strength has saved me.'" God whittled away twenty-two thousand of Gideon's army, but in verse 4, the Lord says to him, "There are still too many men." God tells Gideon to separate the remaining men based on how they drink water from the spring in the desert. As we heard the gurgling water and stood at the small natural spring where Gideon obediently separated his men and was left with only three hundred, the story came alive in a new way.

Gideon was prepared for the battle. He had gathered his resources, used his expertise, and led an enormous army into enemy territory. But we see very clearly in chapter 7 that God did not want Gideon's expertise or his battle plan; God wanted his trust. God wants us to trust him so much that we will do what he tells us, even when it goes against what feels right. God wants our obedience because he fights battles in a way that brings glory to him instead of to us. Gideon had to lay down his faith in his military experience and trust a miracle-working God to fight the battle.

One of the reasons I love the story of Gideon is because I can identify with his fear and his courage. To understand Gideon's humanity even more, we need to go back one chapter to Judges 6, where God chose this young man to free the Israelites from the Midianties who were oppressing and impoverishing God's people, even though the Israelites had a pattern of turning away from him. When an angel of the Lord appeared to Gideon in verse 12, he greeted him with the words, "The LORD is with you, mighty warrior." I can imagine Gideon thinking, *Who me?* The first thing Gideon did was question the angel about God's motives and complain about how God had abandoned them. Let's pick up the story from there:

> The Lord turned to him and said, "Go in the strength you have and save Israel out of Midian's hand. Am I not sending you?"
>
> "Pardon me, my lord," Gideon replied, "but how can I save Israel? My clan is the weakest in Manasseh, and I am the least in my family."
>
> The Lord answered, "I will be with you, and you will strike down all the Midianites, leaving none alive."
>
> Gideon replied, "If now I have found favor in your eyes, give me a sign that it is really you talking to me. Please do

not go away until I come back and bring my offering and set it before you." (vv. 14–17)

I love the whining and doubting and fear we hear in Gideon's quivering voice. Don't we often react this way too? We continue to read that he only truly believes the angel of the Lord, who patiently waits for Gideon to prepare a sacrifice and bake some bread, after he burns up the sacrifice, proving he truly represented the almighty God.

Gideon continued to obey God but with fear and doubt every step of the way. After Gideon was commanded to demolish the altar to Baal, we read, "Gideon took ten of his servants and did as the LORD told him. But because he was afraid of his family and the townspeople, he did it at night rather than in the daytime" (v. 27). His actions caused an uproar, and people were demanding his head! But the spirit of God was upon Gideon, and his life was preserved. Still, Gideon continued to doubt. He asked God to prove himself again.

> Gideon said to God, "If you will save Israel by my hand as you have promised—look, I will place a wool fleece on the threshing floor. If there is dew only on the fleece and all the ground is dry, then I will know that you will save Israel by my hand, as you said." And that is what happened. Gideon rose early the next day; he squeezed the fleece and wrung out the dew—a bowlful of water.
>
> Then Gideon said to God, "Do not be angry with me. Let me make just one more request. Allow me one more test with the fleece, but this time make the fleece dry and let the ground be covered with dew." That night God did so. Only the fleece was dry; all the ground was covered with dew. (vv. 36–40)

Gideon was doing the Texas Two-Step too! He was taking a brave step forward and doubting with every step backward. Nevertheless, God used him to defeat the enemy and help set Israel free, but not without discomfort and risk for Gideon. God had a plan and removed what Gideon thought was necessary for victory. We can't always see or understand why God asks certain things of us or allows us to experience suffering; we don't have a bird's-eye view of the big picture. We can see only the temporary, not the eternal, and we have to trust that the discomfort and uncertainty he is allowing is not only for our good but also for his glory. In this tension, miracles happen.

I found myself asking God for just such a miracle on a hospital visit for my child. We were about to start the first of a yearlong medical treatment for which it's difficult to get insurance authorization as the cost is $12,000 a month. *A month.* That wasn't the only mountain staring us down. We also had acquired a pile of debt from specialist and ER copays, large deductibles, and MRIs and CAT scans.

Sitting in the doctor's office—literally waiting for a call from the insurance company so they could begin—was another low point for me on this road. I was second-guessing our decision to buy a condo, even though our down payment would have covered only part of our annual deductible and the income from it was keeping us afloat. I hated regretting our rainbow in the rain.

In the moment, I felt like my life and our work depended on money rather than God. I don't like that feeling, and I know it's not true. But it's a lie I fall for often. How many times have I thought, *If I just had more money, things would be better*? As we waited for the prized approval, I thought of something another nonprofit founder had recently said to me, "Kristen, one of the reasons we love Mercy House and the way you collaborate with other nonprofits is because you do so from an abundance mindset instead of one of lack." I was honored that was how she viewed our nonprofit because that's a goal. But in the moment, I was operating from a mindset of what we didn't have instead of what we did, and that mindset will dry up miracle ground.

I silently prayed for God to intervene, to be glorified. In other words, I begged for a miracle of healing and provision once again. When the business administrator came in and said, "Not only was this expensive treatment approved; you've also received the highest discount and will only have to pay five dollars a month for the medicine," I cried. Then I cried again, watching my baby receive doses of a drug that sometimes brings dangerous side effects. God provided a miracle of provision, and I was back knocking at his door and asking for protection and healing.

Knowing we wouldn't have to borrow huge amounts of money or mortgage our house to pay for medical treatment eased the burden immensely, but God wasn't done. We had a bill of several thousand dollars at the hospital, and it hung around our necks like a bag of bricks. A day after the insurance company authorized our coverage, there was an envelope on our front porch with the *exact amount* we owed the hospital! Only God! If you lived in our neighborhood, you might have heard Terrell let out a shout of joy.

For each need God has met, there are a dozen more in its place. And how many mountains has he moved that I wasn't even aware of? Job 9:5 tells us, "He moves mountains without their knowing it." How many have melted like wax in the presence of God?

One night I was at dinner with a couple of friends who brought along a stranger to hear the story of Mercy House. For an hour, I talked about how God had wrecked my life, and I answered questions. I cried as I recalled all the impossibilities and miracles along the way and considered the mountains still in front of us. After we ordered dessert, this new friend pulled a prewritten check out of her purse for Mercy House and said, "God will keep doing the impossible. Let's move more mountains together." It was a check for $10,000, and as amazing as it sounds, this has happened more times in the past decade than I can recount. God knew we would need exactly that amount *before* we needed it.

But it doesn't always happen like that. There isn't always a miracle. Usually, there isn't an angel of the Lord with specific instructions, a wet-fleece answer such as Gideon received, an unexpected check from a stranger, or instant healing. Sometimes we see miracles because God uses people to move mountains, and sometimes we see them because he uses mountains to move people.

God really spoke to me through a blog post by author Tricia Lott Williford.

> Nancy Guthrie writes in her book *Hearing Jesus Speak into Your Sorrow*, "Some claim that strong faith is defined by throwing our energies into begging God for a miracle that will take away our suffering and then believing without doubt that He will do it. But faith is not measured by our ability to manipulate God to get what we want; it is measured by our willingness to submit to what He wants."
>
> The truth is, there's no formula we can count on for when Jesus says yes and when He says no. That's the catch

with sovereignty: He gets to decide yes, no, if, when, and how. . . . We can, however, base our confidence on His faithfulness.

Miracles are temporary, but the word of Jesus, His teachings—they bring eternal life. Real life. Your faith in Him, your belief that He is real, even when the miracle isn't yours, even when He doesn't say yes to you—this is what brings eternal life. . . . If we hope for what we do not have, if we believe God is for us, then we can wait patiently for what He has promised. Our ability to endure hardship is almost limitless—if we have the confidence to live in hope.[5]

Isn't that powerful? I love this truth and need the reminder often.

We find Gideon listed in the great faith chapter of Hebrews 11: "Time would fail me to tell of Gideon [and others] who through faith subdued kingdoms, worked righteousness, obtained promises, stopped the mouths of lions, quenched the violence of fire, escaped the edge of the sword, out of weakness were made strong, became valiant in battle, turned to flight the armies of the aliens" (vv. 32–34 NKJV). Hebrews 11 is one of my favorite chapters in the entire Bible. You know it's going to be good when it begins with this definition of faith: "Now faith is the assurance of things hoped for, the conviction of things not seen. For by it the men of old gained approval" (vv. 1–2). In this chapter, we get a rundown of people of faith who died without receiving what God had promised them. Likewise, we aren't going to see every miracle we ask God for, but we still ask, we wait, we pray, we obey, we take one step at a time in the dark, because we know God is faithful. He is good. He is always working.

Maybe I love this epic list because it notes failures as well as successes. We see the untarnished lives of Abel and Enoch, which give us something to aim for, but we can take comfort in the fact that Noah, Abraham, and Sarah also made the list, regardless of their imperfections. We are delighted to find Rahab, Samson, and Gideon on the list because their stories are so unexpected.

I heard a sermon online by Fred Lodge, a pastor at First Baptist Church in Blairsville, Georgia, which was part of a series on the unexpected heroes in Hebrews 11.

> I love the fact that Gideon, while hiding from the Midianites, is approached by an angel of the Lord, who addresses Gideon as "Mighty Hero" (Judg. 6:12 NLT). To which Gideon says (in the Fred Lodge translation), "You mean me???" Then God raised up this same Gideon, the "hiding" hero, to defeat the very people he had earlier been hiding from. . . .
>
> Unexpected? HIGHLY! But not to God, in fact that's exactly the kind of folks He enjoys working with. Need more proof? See Joseph, see Moses, see Esther etc. . . . Which brings me to my next point: I love the fact that the Bible is full of an unlikely cast of characters being raised up by God, and doing great things. AND . . . I love the fact that you and I are in that same category. You and I are God's unexpected heroes for our day and place. We are not wearing cape and mask, but we are dedicated to Him to do what is right, what His will happens to be, at any given time.
>
> Yes, sometimes there are instantaneous miracles along the way. . . . But there is also hard work, faithfulness, bravery in the face of fear, obedience, and a lot of darkness too. Friends, here's the truth we must understand: Jesus is the miracle. His divinity, His Oneness with God, His decision to come

to earth, His sacrifice, His resurrection, His undeniable love for us—He is the miracle.[6]

While the Bible doesn't say it, I like to imagine that in the middle of all those two-steps-forward-and-one-step-backward days the heroes of faith must have faced, there were moments when they too longed for an easy year.

MOUNTAINTOP MOMENT

Corrie Ten Boom, a Dutch writer who helped Jews escape the Nazi Holocaust, says, "Faith sees the invisible, believes the unbelievable, and receives the impossible."[7] We know from what we read in Hebrews 11 and from our own lives that we won't always receive the impossible in this lifetime. But we hope anyway because that is what is regarded as faithfulness—not the arrival, but the journey.

1. Write out your top fears below. Writing them down may help you see they are not as scary as you think. And if they are, you've just added something to your prayer list.
2. Who in Hebrews 11 do you identify with most? Why?
3. What miracles are you asking God for right now?

Journal

11

It's Not Too Late

Desire that your life count for something great!
Long for your life to have eternal significance.
Want this! Don't coast through life without a
passion.

John Piper

I don't remember the exact day I started wearing my mountain necklace, but I remember the day when I decided not to take it off.

It's a tiny, brass mountain-peak charm we sell at Mercy House. I've visited the artisan group in a slum in Kenya where the metal is recycled, melted, and poured into a mold of a tiny mountain. I love that something so small can provide a good job for someone who needs one.

We were eating Pho. But this wasn't just any bowl of the delicious Vietnamese soup. Ally, one of my favorite people on the planet, spent two days lovingly making it. This is the same Ally I wrote about in *Raising World Changers*—the friend who worked for Mercy House and then moved to Thailand to work with one of our artisan partners. She was home for a month after a year overseas, and she invited us to eat Pho with the Pierces, mutual missionary friends who had been living overseas in Tanzania.

It was a sacred night. While we sipped our soup, we talked about the beauty and brokenness of this life. We laughed, remembering the Pierces' premissionary days when our maternity homes were less than a year old in Kenya. We marveled that nearly a decade later, they would be transitioning back to the United States to work at our church and become our missions pastors. We said things at that table that we wouldn't dare share with anyone else.

It was the perfect night—incredible food and amazing fellowship with world changers. These were my people.

And that's the night I decided I wouldn't take off my mountain necklace. The charm hangs next to a tiny charm of Africa. They dangle around my neck and dare me to keep climbing. They also remind me of the importance of changing my view. Sometimes when we stare at the same mountain for too long, we stop seeing the needs around us. It's good to get up, stretch our legs, and step back from our problems so we can see the challenges of others. As my son reminded me, we need to try to see past our own mountains.

This truth became clearer recently after a very bad, no-good week. One of our Mercy House Global artisans, a refugee in Houston, needed to have an emergency C-section. I happened to be in the room visiting when her situation turned urgent. I got home at midnight and slept very little, worrying over this sweet friend and her newborn.

The next morning, I woke up to the flu in full force in my house. I had a miserable pair of feverish, snotty, coughing kids for a week. They literally lay in the same place for days, too achy to move. I had to miss the funeral of a dear friend's mom, who had died in a car accident a few days before. My refugee friend's baby grew more ill. All around, the week made me terribly sad, and I hated that my kids were so sick, that I had to cancel meetings and plans, that I didn't leave the house for days. But our troubles were light and momentary compared to the shadows of the huge mountains in their lives. My own twelve-year-old proved this truth. She was sick, feverish, and pale, but she said, "Mom, how is the baby? Every time I think how bad I feel, I say a prayer for her. Can we pray for her together right now?"

My friend lost her baby that week. As I cared for my family, I felt helpless. Nor was I able to be with my friend who was grieving the loss of her mom. As I passed out Tamiflu and picked up used tissues off the floor, I wanted to do something to help them. My friend Shauna brought over dinner and some groceries for my homebound family, and I knew my friends needed to eat too. *I can set up a meal train*, I thought. With just a few clicks on my phone, we had meals coming to both families. The flu eventually left our house, but our perspective didn't.

Shauna, who has been like Aaron to me, holding up my weary arms during some of my most difficult days, texted this: "Kristen, mountains are miracles disguised as obstacles." She had been Jesus with skin on to me, dropping off groceries and giving encouragement during flu week like it was her job. Yes, if we can look past our troubles, setbacks, and discouragement, then we can see the possibility, the hope in the darkness. It's all in how we look at things, challenging ourselves to rise above the temporary and look for the eternal in our trials. I think this is why James dared us to consider it joy whenever we face trials of many kinds—because God is doing something good in our weakness.

A couple of weeks later, I sat on the edge of a hospital bed and listened to an elderly friend talk about their health. The conversation turned to their life. The clock on the wall ticked its rhythm, but it was regret I heard the loudest. "There are so many things I should have done—*wanted* to do—but I was afraid to take a risk. I played it safe. I didn't say yes to God when he asked. I wasn't always a good person. I got more things wrong than right. And now, it's too late. . . ." Their words trailed off as I watched a single tear fall. I will never forget the remorse and futility of those words, which hung in the air for a long time.

My thoughts of cheering up my elderly friend quickly turned to whispered prayers for wisdom as I tried to form a response. How do you respond to someone's raw, painful words when they are looking in the rearview mirror of their life and wishing the view was different? I knew this person was a Christian and had been successful in the world's eyes with a big career, a big house, and more stuff than you can imagine, but it wasn't money they were referring to. They regretted living the same life year after year. I leaned in, grasped their hand in mine, and said the only thing I could— the only thing that mattered. I spoke the truth: "It's not too late. Your life isn't over. You're still breathing. As long as you have breath, you can do something that matters. You can live each day differently from here on out. You can be brave. You can change your legacy. You can say what needs to be said.

You can share what God has given you. You can change the world by simply meeting the needs of others." By the time I was done, fat tears ran down my cheeks.

I needed to hear the truth ringing in my ears too. Who doesn't need encouragement on our worst days, those filled with regret and remorse for what we could have done, for what we should have said, for who we could have been. Who doesn't wish we had given more, spent less, loved unconditionally? No matter what mountains have impeded our paths, have been ignored, or we've failed to overcome, it's never too late to run our race well. Someone may have cut in on us or maybe we got a little off course sometimes. I spent decades running a race that didn't matter. We can't change the past, but every breath, every new day is a chance to get it right—to live the life God wants us to live.

It's not too late to do that one thing that scares you. It's not too late to say I'm sorry. It's not too late to take a risk. It's not too late to obey God. It's not too late to make today one that you won't regret. I left that hospital room a little sad because remorse will do that to you. But that visit made me a little braver, a little more aware, and a lot more determined to live a life of courage. I couldn't help but think of Robin Sharma's words: "Don't live the same year 75 times and call it a life."[1]

Doing the same thing we've always done leads to a boring and often unsatisfied life. Be brave. Say yes. Do something radical for someone else. Live an adventure. Make this year the one in which you take a risk and ask God to move mountains.

Albert Einstein is broadly credited with saying, "The definition of insanity is doing the same thing over and over again but expecting different results." These challenging words rolled around in my head. When I got home from the hospital, I thought about the strain all this climbing was having on my marriage. We were in an unhealthy cycle of taking the anger and fear of our year out on each other.

I texted my husband the three words that will always scare a spouse half to death: "Can we talk?"

There had been an unspoken tension building; we weren't exactly unhappy, but we also weren't thriving. The stress of life was making us short-tempered and irritable, and we fought over stupid things. We were busy with life and work and weren't resolving the little issues, and they were mounting. We had been married long enough for me to know that marriage is seasonal. There are good seasons when life is steady and outside pressures aren't threatening the ebb and flow of your commitment. Then there are seasons that rock the boat, and if you don't tend to your marriage, it can sink.

Terrell answered, "Sure," and his short answer made me wonder if he was ready for a serious conversation. When a harmless one-word text sends you to the edge, you know it's time for a sit-down.

Except we never sat down because I was standing at the kitchen sink when he came in and said, "What did you want to talk about?"

The kids weren't home and so I blurted, "I want us to stay married for another twenty-five years, and I'm afraid we won't." I barely got the words out before a sob escaped. You could say I caught him off guard, but maybe not; he seemed to know exactly what I was talking about.

"I want to stay married too," he said.

We stood in the kitchen crying and, most importantly, acknowledging the strain this season was putting on our marriage. We gave ourselves permission to feel and say all the things we had bottled up. It wasn't neat or tidy, and we didn't really solve much. But we did verbalize our commitment to each other. We decided that day, standing next to a sink full of dirty dishes, that we would keep working our way back to each other, that we would keep climbing.

I was learning to take the rearview-mirror approach. Half of where we are going is learning from where we've been. I don't want to go down the same path over and over; I want to progress on this journey. It can also be dangerous to forge ahead if we're not learning along the way. Mountain climbing takes a toll on the climbers. If we don't admit this and make provision for self-care on the climb, we will have another avalanche of problems. When our family sets out for a long hike, we pack provisions. We take water and pack food. We stop and rest when the climb is steep. We check on one another. Whenever we take Gunnison, our giant Sheepadoodle, with us, he is the boss of keeping his pack together. The sheepdog in him instinctively wants to herd us. If someone is lagging, he runs back to them and waits. He doesn't leave anyone behind. Sometimes, Emerson takes his leash and runs far ahead, but he stops dead in his tracks if she gets out of view of the rest of us behind. He waits and then drags her back to the group. This is what a rearview-mirror approach looks like—taking breaks, resting, rehydrating with God's Word, climbing in a group, overcoming together.

When we accept the invitation to climb our mountains, we have a choice to make. An invitation isn't a mandate—it isn't forced; it's voluntary participation. We can avoid, neglect, or completely skirt around the mountains in our lives. We can refuse to dream big, do the impossible, dare for the unimaginable. We can wallow and wail our way through disappointments, diagnoses, and disasters. We can overcome or we can barely get by. For many years, I lived the same life every year. I kept the status quo. I didn't risk a lot, but I didn't gain much either. I wasn't incredibly brave, but I wasn't scared either. I didn't serve or give much to other people, but I also didn't experience much purpose or joy.

We have an important decision to make right now. Today. It is this: we can live the same year over and over—maybe ninety times—and call it a life, or we can step out of our comfort zones into the space where miracles happen. We can shake things up. We can say yes to adventure, to the impossible, to something much, much bigger than ourselves. When I stepped over the edge of that terrifying mountain a decade ago, I didn't fall as I feared I would—I flew.

In the middle of that very bad week, I got an email from the Pierces. Lauren wrote:

> Hey, I wanted to share something that I thought you would get . . . and maybe find encouraging. Since coming back to Tanzania, we have been fighting a tick infestation. MAJOR! It's disgusting. Just as I thought we were getting it under control, my house worker called me into our room today and showed me our bedroom window and curtains that were absolutely covered with ticks! I mean covered. Our 3 year old has been sleeping right under this window, and it's an absolute miracle he hasn't had any bite him. Anyway with the heat blazing and ticks crawling, I thought, "I am *so* over Africa!"
>
> And then instantly God in his grace helped me to think. "Wow, Jesus. I am so thankful that you are never 'over' me."

My sin is like the ticks crawling all over my house, but God still wants me and never gives up on me.

I don't know what are in the days ahead. I know life here is very hard, but I also know that God will use these times and is still asking us to embrace this place of ministry. It refines us daily. When we come home, I want to remember these days. I don't want easy, it's just not good for the soul. I think it's going to be challenging, but I'm really looking forward to walking through "hard" with you. Looking forward to fighting for souls together and saying yes to whatever Jesus has in this next stage of ministry.

God wants to use whatever is happening in our lives to bring about the salvation of others. This is always his ultimate goal. When we keep this in mind, it reminds us there is purpose in our pain. We can wallow in the darkness or we can be the light. We can ask him to use our hardships or we can get stuck in only asking why we have trials. Seeing the purpose behind our pain is no small thing—it could ultimately lead to the salvation of others.

Friends, God is near the brokenhearted. I was soaking in my big bathtub the next day. I have this daily habit of filling it as full as possible with water as hot as possible and contemplating life until the water is cold. As I thought, I felt convicted that in my busyness, it had been days since I opened up my Bible. I chastised myself for once again being wishy-washy and not doing what I know needs to be done—not so I can check it off my list but because the Word of God is fresh breath on the stale days you are dying for oxygen. My phone was nearby, and so I opened my Bible app. I sighed because I didn't even know where to start. Where had I left off? Oh, self-condemnation is an enemy that will keep us in one place for too long. I opened it to the verse of the day in the Message version, and here's what it said:

> Jesus was matter-of-fact: "Embrace this God-life. Really embrace it, and nothing will be too much for you. This mountain, for instance: Just say, 'Go jump in the lake'—no shuffling or shilly-shallying—and it's as good as done. That's why I urge you to pray for absolutely everything, ranging from small to large. Include everything as you embrace this God-life, and you'll get God's everything. And when you assume the posture of prayer, remember that it's not all asking. If you have anything against someone, forgive—only then will your heavenly Father be inclined to also wipe your slate clean of sins. (Mark 11:22–25)

I thought of my constant shilly-shallying at the foot of the mountains when I could just say to them, "Go jump in the lake!" Right there in the tub, I prayed about all of it—the burdens in my life and the ones in the lives of others, threatening to cloud my perspective.

MOUNTAINTOP MOMENT

Friends, Jesus cares. He wants us to embrace this life, all of it, because when we accept that our pain is a part of his plan for a greater purpose, nothing will be too much for us.

1. Think about the past year. Is it one you would want to live again and again? Or do you long for something more? What is God inviting you to do?

2. When we take time to look up from our own needs and see what others are going through, it changes our view. How can you see past your own mountains and help carry the burdens of those around you?

3. How can you embrace your life—the parts you don't love, the seasons you wish would end, the burdens that weigh you down?

Journal

12

Do What You Can, Where You Are, with What You Have

Love your neighbor as you love yourself.

Mark 12:31

I don't like making the one-hour drive into Houston alone every month to visit my refugee friends. I mean, I do it, but I enjoy it more when I have someone to talk with on the drive there and process with on the way home.

Nothing interrupts my comfortable life more than visiting the area of my city that holds more than fifty thousand refugees. It's like stepping into another world, and when I step out of it, I tend to bring a bit more of their reality with me. As crazy as it might sound, I ache to be a part of their world.

179

On a recent visit, I talked my family, including Yana, our eighteen-year-old exchange student, into going with me. They really like the chai tea and the people too. Some of my best days are spent in the humble homes of the refugees, drinking delicious tea, tasting foreign foods we've never heard of, struggling to understand one another, and helping them navigate their new city. I'm proud that one of the things Mercy House does locally is provide part-time dignified jobs for a handful of refugee women that open the doors to relationships and empowerment. It's fulfilling.

But I always struggle when I leave because no matter what we do, it isn't enough. The more we love our neighbors, the deeper we are drawn into their lives and their problems. Just this month, I've talked to lawyers about the rights of refugees in our city who aren't being paid fairly, I've been frustrated at potential employers who judge teenaged refugees because of their head coverings, and I've searched for better-paying jobs for them. The more I question, the more questions I have. All my searching and calling haven't solved one of these problems yet. Some days, I wonder if I am making a difference in their lives at all. But then I remember the warmth in my friend's eyes as she bows in respect and refills my tea, and the gratitude on my friends' lips when I pick up handmade items to sell in our retail stores in Texas or put in Fair Trade Friday, and I know I have to keep trying.

On one of these visits a couple of weeks before Christmas, I noticed the clock first. It was the only thing hanging on the bare wall of the home I was sitting in. It wasn't ticking. The hands stood still as if it silently screamed for me to take notice—to see that time was running out. It was my third home visit of the afternoon. My belly was full of chai tea, halal pizza, and a spicy noodle dish I couldn't name (the world wants to feed you), and I'd lost all track of time. I'd stepped over a littered yard, dodged mudholes, climbed stairs, and knocked on the doors of friends from Myanmar, Afghanistan, and Nepal—all relocated to different pockets of my city of Houston.

I sat and sipped and savored the moments in each home with women who have lived such unspeakable horrors that the United Nations deemed them fit for refugee status. It's not a badge any of us would want to wear but don't doubt for a second that it isn't one of honor. In their countries, these families owned homes, drove cars, and had careers, and every bit of their lives changed overnight when persecution and genocide knocked at their front doors. They have lost everything.

Possessions were burned, homes looted, and husbands captured and killed. And now they are my neighbors, and they are starting life over in a new country with a different language, different customs, and untold challenges. Simply put, it is overwhelming. As I stared at the silent clock, it was a very-present reminder that time is running out for many people in our world. As we run around and scoop up last-minute Christmas gifts, hunting for unique finds that will feel just right, for many in the world, the clock is ticking and nothing is right. Women around the globe can count their remaining dollars on one hand; they can feed their children for a couple more nights. They are running out of food, clothes, and rent money. They are running out of time.

When I started Mercy House, I just wanted to help pregnant teens in Kenya. But I quickly learned that when you take a girl out of trafficking, you've also taken away her job, so creating dignified work moved up to the top of our list. We now create dignified jobs not only for those teen moms and their families in Kenya but also for thousands of other women in more than thirty countries around the world through our monthly subscription clubs at Fair Trade Friday. We do this because business is the best way to end poverty.

I handed a bag of supplies to my friend, and she bowed in deep gratitude. We both knew that bag would provide needed money just in time. I glanced again at the clock on the wall and remembered it wasn't working. It reminded me of all the work yet to be done. Talk about mountains.

We visited another home nearby. A young Muslim woman answered our knock and greeted us with a bow. She and her family were expecting us. I reminded them of my name and introduced my family. The young woman at the door translated in broken English to her mother and aunt as her six fatherless siblings filled the room. Both women smiled at the introduction and covered their grins with their hands. We sat on the only furniture in the room and we listened to their story. They arrived in the United States from Afghanistan by way of Pakistan six months ago. Both Afghani women lost their husbands to the Taliban. The four oldest kids, just teenagers, work six days a week for minimum wage to pay for the family of nine to live. We came to meet with them because help from resettlement agencies ends after six months, and these women needed extra work.

Bustling from the small kitchen interrupted my thoughts; I didn't remember seeing a few of the girls get up until they set steaming cups of chai and a halal pizza in front of us. I wasn't really hungry, but I understood what sharing a meal cost them. It was delicious. My husband and younger kids sat on the floor and explained a board game to the children. I watched Madison, home from college for the weekend, chat with our nineteen-year-old interpreter. They talked about university classes—my daughter who attends and her peer who longs to, one a caretaker and the other being taken care of, one from a war zone and the other a comfort zone, one head uncovered and the other wrapped in cloth. These girls from two different worlds, one family who can help another family, were more alike than they knew.

This is my neighbor. The thought hit me hard. G. K. Chesterton says, "We make our friends; we make our enemies; but God makes our neighbor."[1]

I pulled out a bag of cotton yarn and sample washcloths. Their faces lit up and they nodded, and the older of the two women clapped her hands. She wasn't able to work due to health problems, but she could crochet from home and help alleviate the burden. As we walked out the front door, I smiled at the memory of the innocent giggling of the youngest child trying to give my husband a high five. I could still see the wistful longing in the face of the nineteen-year-old as she dreamed of school and still feel the shadow of worry that clung to the widowed sisters.

"Why are people afraid of families like this one?" one of my kids asked from the backseat of the van. It was an important question because the sweetness of our visit was so evident.

"Because they don't know who their neighbors are."

This is my neighbor. We are different, and we are the same. Who is our neighbor? They aren't just friends who look like us, live like we do, love like we choose. Our neighbor is any person we can help.

183

No Reserves, No Retreats, No Regrets

On the way home, the kids challenged me with questions about the fine line between empowering and enabling the marginalized, and we discussed in depth how providing dignified jobs is a healthy solution. But the deeper we dug into the subject, the more questions we had. We were learning that there are unfair employers in our city who underpay and overwork refugees and immigrants, and we can't have everyone making fair-trade product because it's not a sustainable solution. I challenged them to become the kind of people who work to solve these problems. I told them how I wished I had the degree, training, and expertise to make their lives better.

My son caught my eye in the rearview mirror and said, "Mom, you're doing what you can, where you are. You're using what you have, and it matters."

I swallowed the lump in my throat. Sometimes God uses our kids to speak truth right into our hearts. A degree, training, and expertise are incredible tools, and if you have them— or can encourage your kids to get them—use them to change the world! But just because we don't possess them doesn't mean we can't do what we can, where we are, with what we do have.

As we drove back to our comfortable home fifty minutes from the refugee apartments, I looked down at my fair-trade bracelets, which provided jobs. I thought about how my home tells stories of empowerment with its handmade blankets and bowls and the fresh vegetables on the counter, needing to be washed and put away in the fridge, from a local refugee farmer. These small things don't solve the world's problems, but they remind a few people that God hasn't forgotten them.

My son's encouragement reminded me of something I read attributed to Anne Frank: "How wonderful it is that no one has to wait, but can start right now to gradually change the world! How wonderful it is that everyone, great and small, can immediately help bring about justice by giving of themselves."[2]

William Borden was a missionary who died at the age of twenty-five of cerebral meningitis only three months into his Arabic language study in Egypt. He was preparing to take the gospel to an unreached Muslim people group in China. Here's what is written on his tombstone: "Apart from Christ, there is no explanation for such a life."

Isn't that an incredible way to live? These words were found in his Bible: "No reserves. No retreats. No regrets."[3] Your yes may seem small some days, but doing what we can, where we are, with what we have matters! God will take care of the rest. What has he put into your hand? Where has he placed you? What can you do to make someone's life a little better?

Though it may not feel like it some days because we often get bogged down with stuff, chasing the American dream, and visions of success, our deepest and most fulfilling desire is that we will please Jesus and be used by him. This is our purpose as believers—to make the gospel known. As we consider the mountains in our path, we must reflect on how they relate to the gospel. But for me, the gospel has always been a little hard to define, to reduce to a simple definition to live by.

Jeremiah Morris, pastor of Seven Mile Road Church in Houston, led an evangelism seminar at my church. He had an incredible and simple definition of the gospel, and I quickly typed notes from his message on my phone: the gospel can be explained in three succinct truths:

1. We lost it all. The backdrop to the good news is bad news; because of sin, we lost it all.
2. He did it all. Jesus paid our price; he took our place.
3. We get it all. Jesus not only washes away our sins but also makes us righteous; our reward is purpose, contentment, joy in our trials, and everlasting life.

Isn't that a powerful explanation? If we don't know what the gospel is, living it out is challenging and seeing the purpose of our trials is difficult. Morris went on to say, "Evangelism is word and deed that makes Jesus known by loving people. The gospel is news that demands an announcement. Jesus never presented the gospel the same. He met people where they were."[4]

Pastor and author David Platt defines the gospel this way: "The modern-day gospel says, 'God loves you and has a wonderful plan for your life. Therefore, follow these steps, and you can be saved.' Meanwhile, the biblical gospel says, 'You are an enemy of God, dead in your sin, and in your present state of rebellion, you are not even able to see that you need life, much less to cause yourself to come to life. Therefore, you are radically dependent on God to do something in your life that you could never do."[5]

When we understand that the purpose of our mountains—these audacious dreams and difficult challenges—is gospel-related, it alters our approach, our ascending climb, and the setbacks along the way.

It's about the Journey, Not the Destination

Who are we meeting on the climb? How many times have I discovered that life isn't just about the destination; it's also about the journey? The people we meet on the hike are the ones who truly change us, but if we don't pause long enough, sometimes we miss them entirely. For many years, I was trapped in a terrible cycle of living destination to destination, trip to trip, season to season, and I didn't enjoy or cherish the days in between. I was caught up in longing and not living, and it killed my contentment. I know I missed getting to know people along the way, and I didn't really know who my neighbors were.

Who is our neighbor? It could be refugees who need a friend to help them navigate their new life in America, but probably not unless you live in a resettlement city. More than likely, your neighbor is another mom in the car line or a new neighbor who just moved in. Or maybe it's someone on the same unwanted mountain you're on. Without a doubt, some of the medical challenges our family has faced this year have put us in contact with people we would not have met if we weren't enduring this trial. Knowing this truth has helped me to see these encounters in light of the gospel when otherwise it would have been tempting not to look up from the current crisis to see the people in it with me. Some of the seasons I have despised the most have led me to the most incredible people. How can we share truth with them? How can we fulfill God's purpose for us even in our most trying seasons?

Until I started getting out of my comfort zone, I didn't even know people who needed to meet Jesus. I was surrounded by people who looked just like me. In his book *Radical*, David Platt says:

> If we were left to ourselves with the task of taking the gospel to the world, we would immediately begin planning innovative strategies and plotting elaborate schemes. We would organize conventions, develop programs, and create foundations. . . . But Jesus is so different from us. With the task of taking the gospel to the world, he wandered through the streets and byways. . . . All He wanted was a few men who would think as He did, love as He did, see as He did, teach as He did, and serve as He did. All He needed was to revolutionize the hearts of a few, and they would impact the world.[6]

My in-laws have a farm in rural Oklahoma where they raise beef and grow much of their own food. I've walked the rows in the garden with my kids during planting season, and they have wondered how many seeds their grandfather drops into the even rows.

It made me think of the parable of the sower in Matthew 13:1–12:

> That same day Jesus went out of the house and sat by the lake. Such large crowds gathered around him that he got into a boat and sat in it, while all the people stood on the shore. Then he told them many things in parables, saying: "A farmer went out to sow his seed. As he was scattering the seed, some fell along the path, and the birds came and ate it up. Some fell on rocky places, where it did not have much soil. It sprang up quickly, because the soil was shallow. But when the sun came up, the plants were scorched, and they withered because they had no root. Other seed fell among

thorns, which grew up and choked the plants. Still other seed fell on good soil, where it produced a crop—a hundred, sixty or thirty times what was sown. Whoever has ears, let them hear."

The disciples came to him and asked, "Why do you speak to the people in parables?"

He replied, "Because the knowledge of the secrets of the kingdom of heaven has been given to you, but not to them. Whoever has will be given more, and they will have an abundance. Whoever does not have, even what they have will be taken from them."

If we sow liberally, we will reap liberally. If we wait for the perfect time or place or person, we won't reap a harvest. Jesus wants us to make spreading the gospel our way of life. Charles Stanley, pastor and founder of In Touch Ministries, says, "Why do farmers plant their seed? Because they expect to harvest a great deal more than they sow. A single seed that sprouts can yield dozens, scores, even hundreds of seeds. It is the same way with both sin and righteousness—a small decision to do either good or bad reaps a much bigger crop, for either joy or sorrow."[7]

Once I began getting to know people outside of my immediate circle of friends and acquaintances, people who lived differently, ate foods I was eager to try, and worshiped in mosques and temples, it was easier for me to sow more liberally. I was being exposed to different ways of life in my own city, and the more I learned, the more I wanted to know. I think this is a universal truth and not a truth just for diverse cities like mine. There is diversity everywhere—racially, politically, economically, and so on—differences that beckon us to leave our comfort zones, meet our neighbors, and through slow and steady relationships, expose them to the truth of the gospel.

On the first Saturday of 2019, I visited a Sikh temple, a Muslim mosque, a Hindu temple, and a Buddhist temple in Houston. They were less than an hour from my house and all within a few minutes of one another. Terrell and I went with a group that offers temple tours to explain how to build bridges with our international neighbors. Through our work with refugees living in Houston, I am in the homes of women from different cultures every month. I want to know them better and understand what they believe. It was eye-opening, fascinating, intriguing, and very educational. It also made me love my city even more.

Every stop we made had one thing in common, which is also what I loved best and surprised me most: every guru, priest, imam, and leader I met was extremely welcoming, wildly hospitable, and obviously eager for us to understand what they believe and why. We were offered tea and donuts and bottles of water and were invited to "please come back for the free lunch that we offer to the community!" These leaders were kind and intelligent, and they opened the door wide for us to take steps to understand one another.

I met an imam who had gotten his PhD in Islamic studies from Liberia. I watched a Sikh prostrate himself on the ground in his temple to worship. I couldn't help but smile back at the lovely Hindu woman who was so happy to share with our group about higher enlightenment. These were people who look and dress differently than I do—men who don't cut their hair their entire lives, women who cover their heads with a hijab or shave their hair off completely, for example, the beautiful elderly Buddhist woman arranging flowers at an altar.

With the aroma of fragrant incense or foreign food in the air, there were moments I felt as if I were in a different country but I was less than an hour from my front door. Every single person I met was my neighbor. It's so easy to consider those who live on our streets or attend our churches and schools or who have the same skin color we do as our neighbors. And they are, but if we stop there and only love the neighbors who look and act like us, we are not loving all our neighbors.

I saw the following on a T-shirt one day, and I loved it because it's a good definition of who our neighbor is:

Love Thy Neighbor

> Thy Homeless Neighbor
> Thy Muslim Neighbor
> Thy Black Neighbor
> Thy Gay Neighbor
> Thy Immigrant Neighbor
> Thy Jewish Neighbor
> Thy Christian Neighbor
> Thy Atheist Neighbor
> Thy Addicted Neighbor

Our temple tour leader, a man I greatly respect who has spent four decades living and serving in India, Thailand, Pakistan, and Bangladesh, kept referring to himself as a missionary to Houston. He is working to develop relationships and build bridges to people in my city who are unreached and even profiled and stigmatized. People have sometimes referred to me as a missionary because I often go to Kenya. I used to cringe at the word as if it minimized missionaries serving overseas or gave me too much credit. But what if we all started thinking of ourselves as local missionaries in our cities and neighborhoods? Would it help us love our neighbors more? If we saw everyone as our neighbor, we might just see the world differently.

MOUNTAINTOP MOMENT

C. S. Lewis said, "Don't waste time bothering whether you 'love' your neighbor; act as if you did. As soon as we do this we find one of the great secrets. When you are behaving as if you loved someone, you will presently come to love him."[8]

1. Think about what you can do (drive, write, bake), where you are (season, location), with what you have (time, money, resources). With that in mind, how can you share the gospel with those you come in contact with?
2. Who is your neighbor? Make a list.
3. Take your list and tape it to your bathroom mirror or your laptop. Ask God to give you courage to love your neighbors.

Journal

13

The World Needs You

How cool is it that the same God who created
oceans and mountains and galaxies looked at you
and thought the world needed one of you too.

Anonymous

My parents used to say that I had a strong sense of justice. I think I probably just tattled a lot on my siblings, but I have always seen things in black and white. At my worst, this strength looks a little like legalism and a lot like judgment. But when it is used as God intended, I generally rally for the underdog and root for the oppressed. Mom and Dad aren't really surprised that I ended up doing something like Mercy House.

When I first traveled to Kenya and met desperate women who made desperate choices for survival, I quickly understood they didn't need judgment for their decisions to sell one child into slavery to save the others. Rather, they needed justice in their heartbreaking situations.

I've never lived a day without the privilege of choice, so I can't imagine what it's like to have no choices at all. But when I look through the eyes of compassion, I wonder if I would have made the same desperate sacrifices they had. I understood the words of Solon: wrongdoing can only be avoided "if those who are not wronged feel the same indignation at it as those who are."[1]

When I first read the following words, they caught my attention. When I learned they were from Chief Justice John Roberts to his son and classmates, I was surprised. When I discovered they were part of a commencement speech to an entitled group of graduates, I was delighted. They are important, necessary words that we all need to hear. They aren't said in judgment; they are said in love.

> From time to time in the years to come, I hope you will be treated unfairly so that you will come to know the value of justice. I hope that you will suffer betrayal because that will teach you the importance of loyalty. . . . I hope you will be lonely from time to time so that you don't take friends for granted. I wish you bad luck, again, from time to time so that you will be conscious of the role of chance in life and understand that your success is not completely deserved and that the failure of others is not completely deserved either. . . . I hope you will have just enough pain to learn compassion.[2]

As a parent, I cheered his words. As a human, I winced at their truth. I didn't know the pain of the world until I compared it to the ease of my life. I didn't know to appreciate my choices until I met women who had none. Can we know the beauty of happiness until we've tasted a bit of sorrow? Can we know the height of success unless we have tasted the depth of loss? Can we truly appreciate the miracles if we haven't first faced the mountains? It's in our loss that we come to understand our gain. In the past decade, I have learned these truths on a deeper level. As taxing and trying as mountain climbing is, I'm thankful for what God has taught me.

Light in the Darkness

Google has also taught me a lot. I admit it; I'm an avid googler. If I haven't heard of a term or have a question about, well, anything, I go to Google. I have diagnosed quite a few things that way or accidentally scared myself half to death. And it has been handy a few times. On one of my trips to Kenya, I was concerned about a baby and a teen mom, and I mentioned it to staff there after a quick Google consultation. Twice, doctors confirmed my suspicions and made a diagnosis of something rather serious. One of our staff looked at me afterward, shaking his head and saying, "Are you also a medical doctor?"

I laughed. "Oh, no, I just have Google, but I also think it was a lucky guess," I answered. I do not recommend self-diagnosis, and I'm not proud that my quest for knowledge sometimes also sends me into panic mode.

When we were facing a serious illness, I resisted the urge to google causes and treatments. My willpower lasted for about twenty minutes. My search gave me some solid answers, but it also made me very fearful of the only approved treatment. In the past year, I've lost count of how many doctors' appointments we've been to and how much waiting we have done. On one of these visits, while we waited and hoped for a good report, I thought to myself, *If there's bad news again, I don't think I can make my way through the darkness.* But as soon as the words formed in my mind, I reminded myself that even in the darkness, the light gets in. Jesus has taught me I don't need to fear the dark anymore because he is lighting the way.

How do we ask God for something when our last prayer is still unanswered? It might feel as if our prayers don't matter to him, or he isn't listening. What do we do? We pray anyway because we are changed when we do, regardless of the outcome. We lean into Isaiah 55:8: "'For my thoughts are not your thoughts, neither are your ways my ways,' declares the Lord. 'As the heavens are higher than the earth, so are my ways higher than your ways and my thoughts than your thoughts.'"

Within two months of the diagnosis, I was begging God to provide a way for us to get the very treatment that terrified me. Suddenly, I was grateful for the thing I was most afraid of—and that is how I feel about the mountains behind me.

It can be overwhelming to face a mountain we want to climb or one we don't. We have more questions than answers, and the unknown outweighs the known. We are afraid. But when we stand at the top or on the other side of it, we see that mountain in a completely different way. One day, we might even be able to thank God for it.

There are countless mountains in my rear view, and they stand as memorials of what God has done in the past and as reminders of what God will do in the future. I love these strong, beautiful words from Christine Caine: "God is faithful. He'll fulfill every promise he's made. There's no disease God cannot heal, no heart he cannot mend, no bondage he cannot break, no enemy he cannot defeat, no mountain he cannot move, and no need he cannot meet. And because that same Spirit lives inside each of us, we move forward undaunted. . . . Focus on our unshakeable God instead of the chaos around you, and he will carry you through the challenges and on to victory."[3]

And what is our victory exactly? I used to believe it was a perfect life. Or if I just had enough time, enough money, enough people, enough resources, I would feel victorious. But the destination isn't our victory; faith is the victory, and not faith in the outcome or faith in another person because people will let us down. Faith in Jesus is our victory.

I was riding with my friend Shauna to a local coffee shop, and we were talking about the "easy days" I dream of. She reminded me what true victory looks like: "Keep the faith because faith IS the victory. Not faith in xyz or faith in the hope that xyz will happen. It's faith in Jesus. I don't believe because I see. I don't stop believing because I don't see."

If Jesus doesn't move the mountain or perform the miracle, he is still good. We praise him when he does the impossible, and we praise him when he doesn't.

Later, Shauna texted me Habakkuk 3:17–19: "Though the fig tree may not blossom, nor fruit be on the vines; though the labor of the olive may fail, and the field yield no food; though the flock may be cut off from the fold, And there be no herd in the stalls—yet I will rejoice in the LORD, I will joy in the God of my salvation. The LORD God is my strength; . . . And He will make me walk on my high hills" (NKJV).

Following the Scripture passage was this loving admonishment:

> Where are the hills found? On mountains! Even though everything looks hopeless and helpless and barren and short of the resources we need—though nothing seems to be working as it should or how we want or need it to—though sustaining resources are absent or in short supply—YET I will rejoice! He will make my feet able to navigate even the riskiest, most dangerous terrain. That mountain—the rocky terrain is encountered as you scale the mountain to get to the other side, and it's not until you get to the rocky, scary, next-step-could-be-death terrain that you discover the hinds' feet God has supplied for high places as he takes you over the mountain to the other side.

I have amazing friends. Isn't that a beautiful word? It reminded me of the book *Hinds' Feet on High Places* by Hannah Hurnard that I read as a teenager. I love the way Amazon describes it: "A timeless allegory dramatizing the yearning of God's children to be led to new heights of love, joy, and victory. In this moving tale, follow Much-Afraid on her spiritual journey as she overcomes many dangers and mounts at last to the High Places. There she gains a new name and is transformed by her union with the loving Shepherd."[4]

The Shepherd explains to Much-Afraid what the "High Places" are:

> "The High Places," answered the Shepherd, "are the starting places for the journey down to the lowest place in the world. When you have hinds' feet and can go 'leaping on the mountains and skipping on the hills,' you will be able, as I

am, to run down from the heights in the gladdest self-giving and then go up to the mountains again. You will be able to mount to the High Places swifter than eagles, for it is only up on the High Places of Love that anyone can receive the power to pour themselves down in an utter abandonment of self-giving."[5]

Much-Afraid (let's call her Kristen) responds in my favorite quote from the book:

> Therefore I begin to think, my Lord, you purposely allow us to be brought into contact with the bad and evil things that you want changed. Perhaps that is the very reason that we are here in this world, where sin and sorrow and suffering and evil abound, so that we may let you teach us so to react to them, that out of them we can create lovely qualities to live forever. That is the only really satisfactory way of dealing with evil, not simply binding it so that it cannot work harm, but whenever possible overcoming it with good.[6]

In our culture and in our own carnal thinking, we often equate a successful climb with a successful outcome. But the results don't dictate our achievements—faithfulness does.

This Is about Obedience

Years ago, in the very early years of starting Mercy House and daring to climb this massive mountain, I spent an hour with an investor, spilling out stories and words and very non-businesslike tears because I thought this might be the answer to my constant money-raising questions, hand-wringing, and overthinking. Maybe this was the moment I could let out the breath I'd been holding for years.

He closed his leather portfolio, clasped his hands together, and slowly placed them on it—all businesslike. He then leaned across the table and crushed my brave yes with these words: "You've told me your story and shown me a business model you can never sustain. How will you define if Mercy House Global is ever really successful?"

Those words knocked the breath out of me and left me gasping and grasping because instead of blank checks and paper miracles slid across the table, there was doubt and discouragement. For a split second, I almost believed the despair he spoke over our life's work. We were inexperienced and inadequate, unqualified and unsure.

Since our first yes, we have been overwhelmed and in over our heads with broken girls, horrific stories of survival, and so much grief and sorrow. It has been years of two steps forward and sometimes three steps back. So what gave us the audacity to fund rescues of abused pregnant teens in Kenya and to create jobs in thirty other countries for oppressed and impoverished women?

God, that's who.

That day years ago, I stacked my papers in a neat pile, took a deep breath, and said with righteous indignation: "This isn't about success. It's about obedience. It might not look profitable on paper, but most supernatural things don't. And that first baby born alive in 2011 is how we define success."

I have thought about that meeting probably a thousand times. I have marveled at how God has provided money and miracles at every turn. It has been hard and holy work. No, we aren't big, but God is, and together, we are changing the world. Most days, it feels as though what we do is insignificant because for every girl we help, a hundred more wait for rescue. For every baby born alive, there are countless lost. For every job we provide, there are still thousands of women who put their children to bed hungry every night. Every success has been built on the devastation of failure. We are in the people business and it is messy, but it matters.

You were made to move mountains. It is your purpose, your destiny. God created you to do what no one else can accomplish. He takes your unique gifts, your personality, and your past, and he places you in a position to do something only you can do. Your faith will increase on the climb. It will be hard and discouraging, overwhelming and difficult, but it will be worth it. It matters. It's the starfish story again and again. We can't toss all the dying starfish washed up on the shore back into the ocean, but we can throw a few. It might seem insignificant—until you ask those that are alive in the ocean.

MOUNTAINTOP MOMENT

Ann Voskamp said in her book *The Way of Abundance*, "You may believe in God, but never forget—it's God who believes in you. Every morning that the sun rises and you get to rise? That's God saying He believes in you, that He believes in the story He's writing through you. He believes in you as a gift the world needs."[7]

1. Your story isn't over. We don't have to know what the next chapter will be, but think about what is on your next page.

2. What is the next right step you can take today toward your mountain?

3. God believes in you. He wants you to believe in yourself. You're alive today because there is a purpose for today. There is someone who needs your kindness, your obedience. Fill in the blank and say it out loud, "God, my purpose for today is to _____.

Journal

Epilogue

Beyond Mountains, There Are Mountains

I visited Haiti a few years ago and found it to be a beautiful island covered in mountains. When a friend, who lives and works there, included this Creole proverb *Deye mon gen mon* in an email to me as I was wrapping up this book, I immediately saw its double meaning. The proverb means "Beyond mountains, there are mountains." People who know and love Haiti understand that this popular saying is referring to more than topography and mountain views. It also implies that in this poverty-filled, often tumultuous country, when you solve one problem there is always another that must also be solved.

I don't know why this proverb was such an epiphany for me. It seems quite obvious if you've ever stood on a mountaintop: you're likely going to see other mountains around and beyond it. But I think it hit me between the eyes because of the relentless hope I've had for a view without mountains.

God used this proverb to remind me that there are no seasons exclusively easy; there are no windfalls or shortcuts. When we care about what God cares about, when we stand for justice, the life God calls us to will be hard. It's extremely beautiful, breathtaking even, but still hard. Don't let anyone tell you that following Jesus will be comfortable. Don't believe for a second that being a Christian will be easy. Following Jesus won't cost us just something—it will cost us everything.

I think you know this about me by now: I struggle with this truth. I wrestle with what God has asked me to do. Before the climb, we did not know how difficult it would be. God spares us from seeing the highest highs and lowest lows because we probably couldn't handle the views. If I'd known how hard or how high the climb would be, I wonder if my sinfulness and selfishness would have convinced me to stay at the base.

Sometimes people will ask me for advice about starting a nonprofit or beginning a challenging climb. This is what I usually say: "My best advice, before you begin something completely new, is to try to find someone who is already doing what you want to do and join them on their climb. Pool your resources, share the burden. It's possible they feel like they are drowning, and you could be the answer to their prayers."

I also remind people not to wish to be in someone else's shoes; don't long for their mountain. The view is never as good as you imagine. Because beyond the mountains, there are more mountains. The view makes me long for Jesus to return and make things right in this world.

But then I read these bold words from Elisabeth Elliot, wife of Jim Elliot, a missionary killed in Ecuador, and I am moved to continue climbing even in my hardships: "A whole lot of what we call 'struggling' is delayed obedience."[1]

I am often simultaneously filled with hope and despair. I'm all in, but some days what feels like 50 percent working and 50 percent quitting is really 100 percent surrendering.

The day before I was to fly out of the country recently, I was filled with remorse for booking the ticket and planning the trip because I felt weak and inadequate, overwhelmed and afraid of the journey. I kept thinking, *I can't. I can't. I can't.*

The next day, as I sat in the plane on the tarmac, waiting to take off, I saw a cartoon on Instagram of a lady with conversation bubbles surrounding her. Every one of them read, "I can't."

But the caption read, "I am."

This perfectly sums me up. I constantly feel as if I can't continue on the mountain, climbing to new heights, but I *am* because God is with me. I can. *We can.* C. S. Lewis wrote in a letter, "Relying on God has to begin all over again every day as if nothing had yet been done."[2]

Yes, beyond mountains, there are mountains, but for the first time in nearly a decade, I'm okay with that. I believe God will continue to move the mountains of our dreams and disasters. Because this is who he is, and this is what he does.

So, friends, climb. Your words, your mission, your gifts, your dreams, your failures, and *you* matter. Chase the dreams in your heart and overcome the obstacles in your way because the world needs you. You were made to move mountains.

Journal

Acknowledgments

To Terrell: I wrote this book during our twenty-fifth year of marriage, and I think we can both agree the year was a challenging one. I'm thankful for our commitment to each other—no matter how high the mountains or how hard the climb in this life. I love you. I'm glad that no matter what we face, we face it together. Thanks for enduring with this Strategic INFJ Enneagram 1. We both know I can be extra.

To my children: I have watched each of you scale some difficult mountains in your short lives, and you have done so with grace, tenacity, and much courage. I love you, Madison, and the way you are embracing college life. I have been amazed at your personal growth and leadership and the way you move mountains. Jon-Avery, I can't believe your senior year is here. I can't wait to see where your kindness, maturity, hard work, and love for others take you. I love you! Emerson, how is my baby a teenager? I love your bravery in trying new things, and your compassion for others inspires me. Soon, it will just be the three of us at home, and I look forward to that special time together. I love you!

To Shauna: I didn't know how much I needed you in my life until you showed up and stayed. The way you have loved, supported, and encouraged me has been one of the greatest acts of generosity I've ever experienced. Thank you for loving me so well, for praying me through this difficult year, and for holding up my weary arms when I couldn't.

To Ann: No one will ever really know how much our texting conversations have inspired, encouraged, and challenged me while I wrote this book. Thank you for giving me a safe place to be vulnerable and for linking arms with me in this work to support our sisters around the globe. I love the way you change the world.

To my Kenyan family: We painted mountains together (which became the cover of this book!). Thank you for your example. My world is better because you are in it. You make me want to never give up.

To my sister, Kara: You are my person. I love you, and I'm grateful we are there for each other.

To my parents and my in-laws: Thank you for loving me! I love you.

To the Mercy House staff: Thanks for letting me cry every day at work. You come to work every week with joy and purpose, and you treat your job as if it's a mission—because it is. You're the best mountain movers I know! I love y'all.

To my blog readers: We've been through a lot together in the last decade. You know me well, and you're still here. Thank you for everything.

To Bill Jensen, my agent: Thank you for believing in me.

To the Baker Books team: This book happened because you were patient with me. Thanks for the extension! You turned this somewhat difficult-for-me project into a relief!

Notes

Introduction

1. Kristen Welch, *Rhinestone Jesus* (Carol Stream, IL: Tyndale, 2014), 35.

Chapter 1 The Mountain in Our Way

1. Vera Nazarian, *The Perpetual Calendar of Inspiration* (Highgate Center, VT: Norilana Books, 2010).

2. Paul Washer of HeartCry Missionary, "Slip Away and Be with God," I'll Be Honest, September 4, 2010, https://illbehonest.com/slip-away-and-be-with -god-paul-washer.

3. Welch, *Rhinestone Jesus*, 57–58.

4. Quoted in Welch, *Rhinestone Jesus*, 53.

5. Colin Powell, Good Reads, accessed August 4, 2019, https://www.good reads.com/quotes/313423-a-dream-doesn-t-become-reality-through-magic-it -takes-sweat.

6. A. W. Tozer, *A Leader's Heart* (Nashville: Thomas Nelson, 2010), 134.

7. Louie Giglio, *Goliath Must Fall: Winning the Battle Against Your Giants* (Nashville: Thomas Nelson, 2017), 15.

8. Jarrid Wilson, "God Uses Flawed People to Share Hope to a Flawed World," jarridwilson.com, March 16, 2014, jarridwilson.com/god-uses-flawed-people-to -share-hope-to-a-flawed-world/.

9. David Brooks, *The Second Mountain: The Quest for a Moral Life* (New York: Random House, 2019), xxii.

10. Brooks, *The Second Mountain*, xxxiii.

Chapter 2 Rejoicing in the Impossible

1. Kristen Welch, *Raising World Changers in a Changing World* (Grand Rapids: Baker Books, 2018), 49–50.

213

2. Kevin G. Harney, *Reckless Faith: Embracing a Life without Limits* (Grand Rapids: Baker Books, 2012), 18.

3. O. R. Melling, *The Summer King* (New York: Amulet Books, 2007), 246.

Chapter 3 The Best View Means the Hardest Climb

1. Kristen Welch, "Hey Mom, Your Kids Are Going to Be Okay," *We Are THAT Family* (blog), January 29, 2019, http://wearethatfamily.com/2019/01/hey-mom-your-kids-are-going-to-be-okay/.

2. William Drysdale, *Proverbs from Plymouth Pulpit: Selected from the Writings and Sayings of Henry Ward Beecher* (New York: D. Appleton and Company, 1887), 56.

3. Francis Chan, *The Francis Chan Collection: Crazy Love, Forgotten God, Erasing Hell, and Multiply* (Colorado Springs: David C. Cook, 2014), 88.

4. John Eldredge, *Moving Mountains: Praying with Passion, Confidence, and Authority* (Nashville: Thomas Nelson, 2016), 241.

5. Shane Claiborne and Tony Campolo, *Red Letter Revolution: What If Jesus Really Meant What He Said?* (Nashville: Thomas Nelson, 2012), 33.

6. Kristen Welch, "When You're Just About to Give Up (An Urgent Request)," *We Are THAT Family* (blog), July 23, 2018, https://wearethatfamily.com/2018/07/when-youre-just-about-to-give-up-an-urgent-request/.

7. Katherine J. Butler, *Habits of the Heart: 365 Daily Exercises for Living like Jesus* (Carol Stream, IL: Tyndale, 2017), 255.

8. Charles Wentworth Upham, *The Life of Washington, in the Form of an Autobiography*, vol. 2 (Boston: Marsh, Capen, Lyon, and Webb, 1840), 181.

Chapter 4 Jesus Changes Everything

1. Joe Paprocki, "What Is the Significance of Mountains in the Bible?," Busted Halo, October 12, 2018, https://bustedhalo.com/ministry-resources/what-is-the-significance-of-mountains-in-the-bible/.

2. "Q&A with Francis Chan: Letters to the Church," Christian Post, August 31, 2018, https://www.christianpost.com/voice/qa-with-francis-chan-letters-to-the-church.html.

3. Francis Chan, "Is Suffering Optional?," Preach It, Teach It, accessed July 24, 2019, https://www.preachitteachit.org/fileadmin/SiteFiles/LegacyUploads/Microsoft_Word_-_Is_suffering_optional_Chan.pdf.

4. Ann Voskamp, Facebook, November 15, 2018, https://www.facebook.com/AnnVoskamp/posts/turns-out-all-our-homes-tell-a-story-our-homes-are-always-either-telling-fair-tr/2270530016292493/.

5. Todd Phillips, *Keep Climbing Leader's Guide* (Richardson, TX: Bluefish TV, 2010), 36, http://www.thesummitchurch.net/wp-content/uploads/Keep-Climbing-Leaders-Guide.pdf.

6. Phillips, *Keep Climbing*, 25.

7. Phillips, *Keep Climbing*, 26.

8. Richard Dahlstrom, *The Colors of Hope: Becoming People of Mercy, Justice, and Love* (Grand Rapids: Baker Books, 2011), 15.

Chapter 5 Oh, We of Little Faith

1. Mother Teresa, *A Call to Mercy: Hearts to Love, Hands to Serve*, ed. Brian Kolodiejchuk (New York: Crown Publishing Group, 2016), 6.

2. Kristen Welch, "Welcome Home," *We Are THAT Family* (blog), August 16, 2018, https://wearethatfamily.com/2018/08/welcome-home-2/.

3. Sandra Kring, Good Reads, accessed July 24, 2019, https://www.goodreads.com/quotes/684737-the-tiny-seed-knew-that-in-order-to-grow-it.

4. Joel Osteen, *It's Your Time* (New York: Howard Books, 2009), 142.

5. Eldredge, *Moving Mountains*, 14.

Chapter 6 Permission to Grieve

1. Timothy Keller, *Walking with God through Pain and Suffering* (New York: Riverhead Books, 2013), 3.

2. Keller, *Walking with God*, 180–81.

3. Hillsong Worship, "Broken Vessels (Amazing Grace)," written by Joel Houston and Jonas Myrin, track 3 on live album *No Other Name* (2014).

4. Christine Caine, *Unexpected: Leave Fear Behind, Move Forward in Faith, Embrace the Adventure* (Grand Rapids: Zondervan, 2018), 72.

5. Christine Caine, *Undaunted: Daring to Do What God Calls You to Do* (Grand Rapids: Zondervan, 2012), chap. 4, emphasis original.

6. Christine Caine, *Unstoppable: Running the Race You Were Born to Win* (Grand Rapids: Zondervan, 2014), 84–85.

7. Ann Voskamp, Facebook, February 7, 2019, https://www.facebook.com/AnnVoskamp/posts/2383619631650197.

8. Bible Trivia, *A Voice in the Wilderness*, accessed July 24, 2019, http://www.a-voice.org/trivia/009.htm.

9. Tim Keller (@timkellernyc), Twitter, January 19, 2019, 8:30 a.m., https://twitter.com/timkellernyc/status/1086662169742266382.

Chapter 7 Your Invitation to Climb

1. Mark Udall Quotes, Brainy Quotes, accessed July 25, 2019, https://www.brainyquote.com/quotes/mark_udall_505410.

2. Eldredge, *Moving Mountains*, 4, 5, 7.

3. Eldredge, *Moving Mountains*, 40.

4. Eldredge, *Moving Mountains*, 48–49, emphasis original.

5. Oswald Chambers, *Prayer: A Holy Occupation* (Grand Rapids: Discovery House, 1992), introduction.

Chapter 8 Just Keep Climbing

1. Anne Lamott, *Bird by Bird: Some Instructions on Writing and Life* (New York: Anchor Books, 1995), xxiii.

2. Jill Herzig, "Kids Growing Up: How Wonderful and How Sad," *Redbook*, May 13, 2013.

3. Trillia Newbell, *Fear and Faith: Finding the Peace Your Heart Craves* (Chicago: Moody, 2015), 125.

4. Thomas Bowen, interview with Trillia Newbell, Radical, April 1, 2015, https://radical.net/articles/fear-and-faith.

5. Bowen, interview with Newbell.

6. Mosaic MSC, "Tremble," written by Andres Figueroa, Hank Bentley, Mariah McManus, and Mia Fieldes, track 6 on live album *Glory & Wonder* (2016).

7. Wikipedia, s.v. "Death zone," last modified June 16, 2019, https://simple.wikipedia.org/wiki/Death_zone.

8. Lifeway Women's Study Bible (Nashville: B&H, 2015), 1584.

9. Krishnadev Calamur, "Who Are Nepal's Sherpas?," NPR, April 22, 2014, https://www.npr.org/sections/parallels/2014/04/22/305954983/who-are-nepals-sherpas.

10. Ann Voskamp, Facebook, January 3, 2017, https://www.facebook.com/annvoskamp/photos/A.369461463066034/2341437019201792/?TYPE=3&Theater.

11. Anne Radmacher, "Courage Doesn't Always Roar," *Mary Anne EM Radmacher EManates* (blog), June 23, 2016, https://www.maryanneradmacher.net/apps/blog/show/44046084-courage-doesn-t-always-roar.

Chapter 9 Rainbows in the Rain

1. Chip Gaines, *Capital Gaines* (Nashville: Thomas Nelson, 2017), 165–66.

2. Welch, *Rhinestone Jesus*, xvii.

Chapter 10 Miracle Territory

1. Priscilla Shirer (@PriscillaShirer), Twitter, April 16, 2012, 8:07 a.m., https://twitter.com/priscillashirer/status/191905601947828224?prefetchTimestamp=1566739090464.

2. Christine Caine, Facebook, December 5, 2015, https://www.facebook.com/theChristineCaine/posts/10156388425365089.

3. Merriam-Webster, s.v. "miracle," accessed July 29, 2019, https://www.merriam-webster.com/dictionary/miracle.

4. John Piper, *Taste and See* (New York: Crown Publishing Group, 2016), 302–3.

5. Tricia Lott Williford, "When Everyone Else Is Getting Their Miracle: How to Deal with Feeling Overlooked," guest post on Ann Voskamp's blog, July 10, 2017, https://annvoskamp.com/2017/07/when-everyone-else-is-getting-their-miracle-how-to-deal-with-feeling-overlooked/.

6. Fred Lodge, "The Blind Man," March 12, 2017, sermon at First Baptist Church, Blairsville, GA, https://www.fbcvision.com/resources/sermons1/unexpe.

7. Corrie Ten Boom, *Jesus Is Victor* (Old Tappan, NJ: Fleming H. Revell, 1985), 184.

Chapter 11 It's Not Too Late

1. Robin Sharma, Facebook, June 3, 2016, https://www.facebook.com/RobinSharmaOfficial/photos/dont-live-the-same-year-75-times-and-call-it-a-life/10154183314955040/.

Chapter 12 Do What You Can, Where You Are, with What You Have

1. Gilbert K. Chesterton, *The Essential Gilbert K. Chesterton* (New York: Simon & Schuster, 2013), 196.

2. Anne Frank, "Give!," in *Anne Frank's Tales from the Secret Annex* (New York: Bantam 2003), n.p.

3. Tim Challies, *Devoted: Great Men and Their Godly Moms* (Minneapolis: Cruciform Press, 2018), 60.

4. Jeremiah Morris, Evangelism Training at Church Project, Spring, Texas, January 13, 2019.

5. David Platt, *Radical: Taking Back Your Faith from the American Dream* (Colorado Springs: Multnomah, 2010), 32.

6. Platt, *Radical*, 87–88.

7. Charles F. Stanley, "Life Principle 6: The Principle of Sowing and Reaping," In Touch Ministries, July 6, 2014, https://www.intouch.org/Read/life-principle-6 -the-principle-of-sowing-and-reaping.

8. C. S. Lewis, *Mere Christianity*, rev. and enlarged ed. (New York: Harper-One, 2015), 132.

Chapter 13 The World Needs You

1. F. A. Paley, *Greek Wit* (London: George Bell and Sons, 1881), 37.

2. Katie Reilly, "'I Wish You Bad Luck.' Read Supreme Court Justice John Roberts' Unconventional Speech to His Son's Graduating Class," *Time*, July 5, 2017, http:// time.com/4845150/chief-justice-john-roberts-commencement-speech-transcript/.

3. Jonathan Peterson, "How to Find Unshakeable Strength in the Bible: An Interview with Christine Caine," *Bible Gateway Blog*, November 21, 2017, https:// www.biblegateway.com/blog/2017/11/how-to-find-unshakeable-strength-in-the -bible-an-interview-with-christine-caine/.

4. Hannah Hurnard, *Hinds' Feet on High Places* (Carol Stream, IL: Tyndale, 1979), https://www.amazon.com/Hinds-Feet-Places-Hannah-Hurnard/dp/0842 314296.

5. Hannah Hurnard, *Hinds' Feet on High Places* (New York: Simon & Schuster, 2013), chap. 4.

6. Hurnard, *Hinds' Feet on High Places*, chap. 4.

7. Ann Voskamp, *The Way of Abundance* (Grand Rapids: Zondervan, 2018), 47.

Epilogue

1. Elisabeth Elliot, "Leaving Self Behind," *Revive our Hearts* (podcast), September 27, 2013, https://www.reviveourhearts.com/podcast/revive-our-hearts /leaving-self-behind-elisabeth-elliot/.

2. C. S. Lewis, *Letters of C. S. Lewis*, ed. W. H. Lewis and Walter Hooper, reissue ed. (New York: HarperOne, 2017), 455.

Kristen Welch is the creator of the popular parenting blog *We Are THAT Family* (www.wearethatfamily.com), has a regular column in *ParentLife* magazine, and is a frequent radio guest and speaker. Author of *Raising World Changers in a Changing World*, Kristen is the founder of Mercy House Global and lives with her family in Texas.

Connect with

KRISTEN

WEARETHATFAMILY.COM

WeAreThatFamily

TUNE IN TO KRISTEN'S
MOVING MOUNTAINS
PODCAST

AVAILABLE ON APPLE PODCASTS OR
WHEREVER YOU GET YOUR PODCASTS.